This Book Belongs To

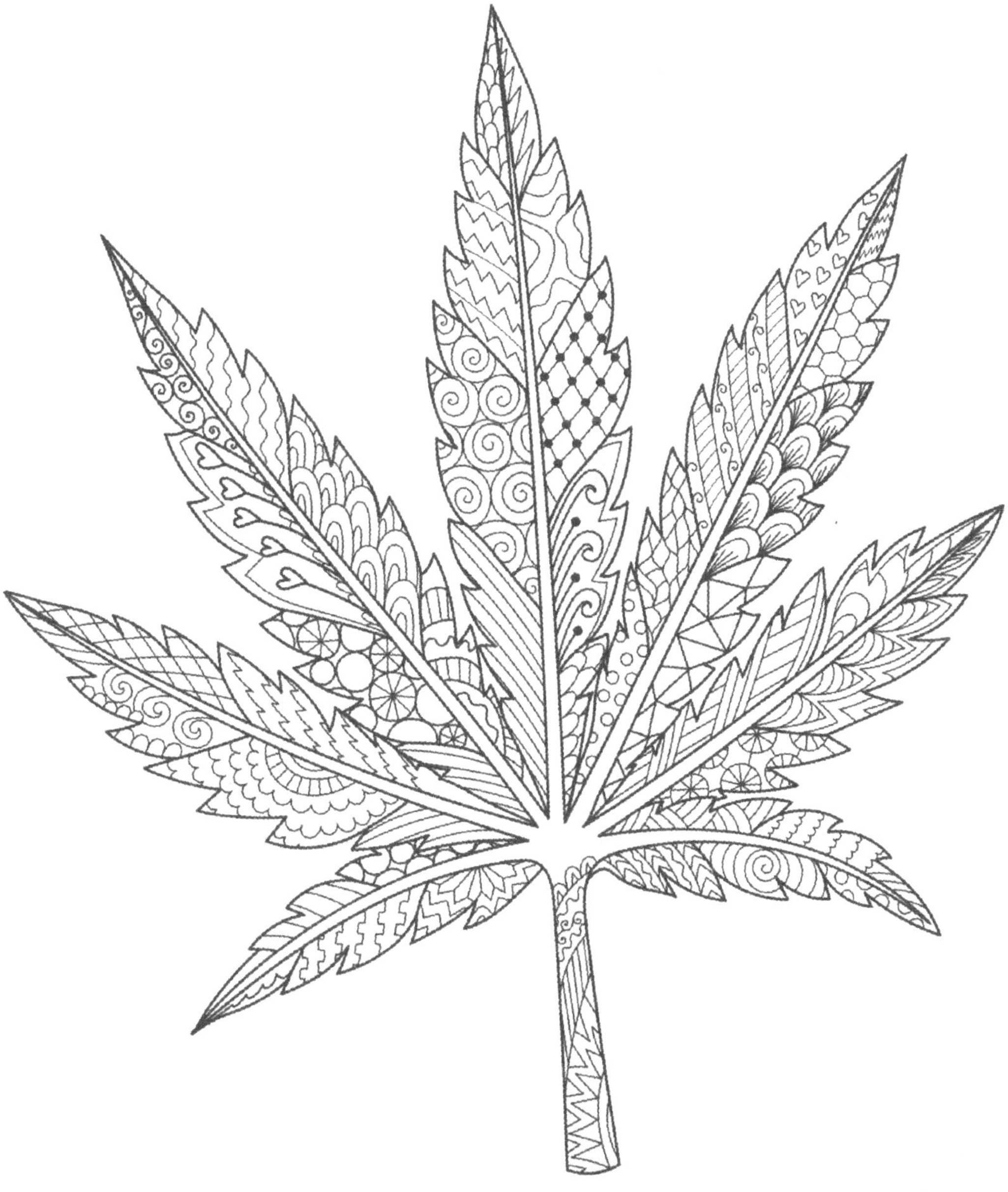

FIRST EDITION

ISBN 9798720914998

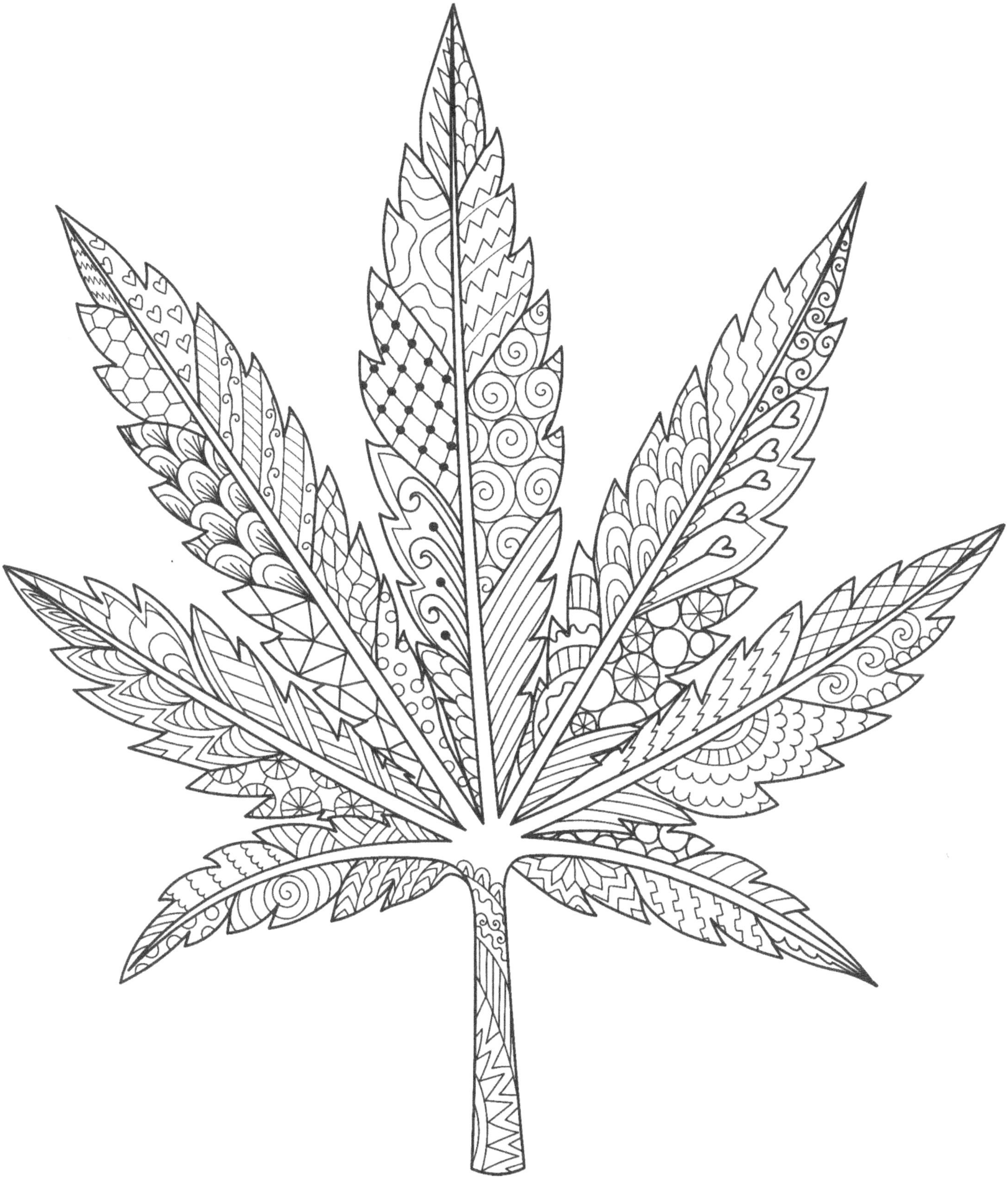

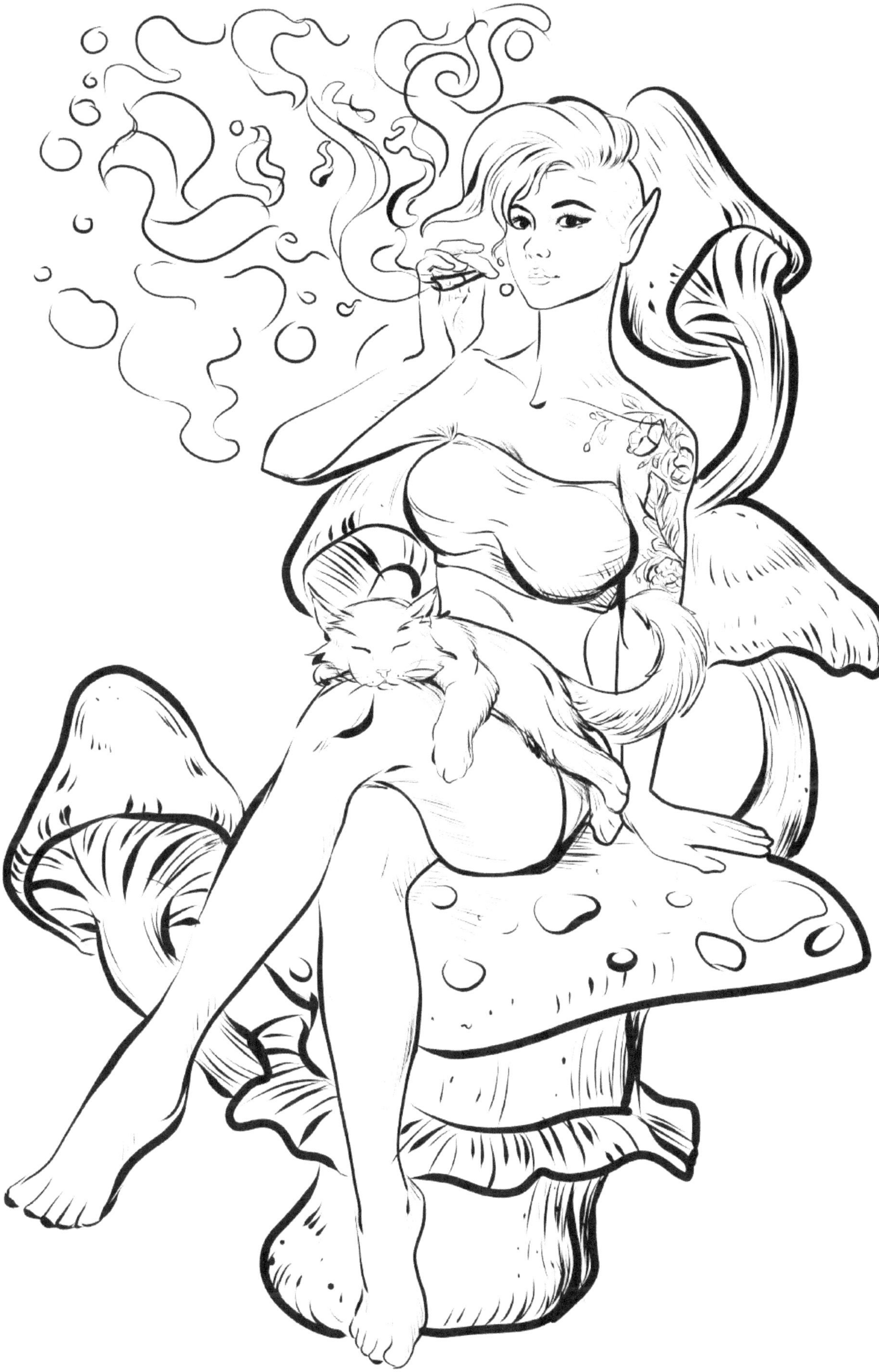

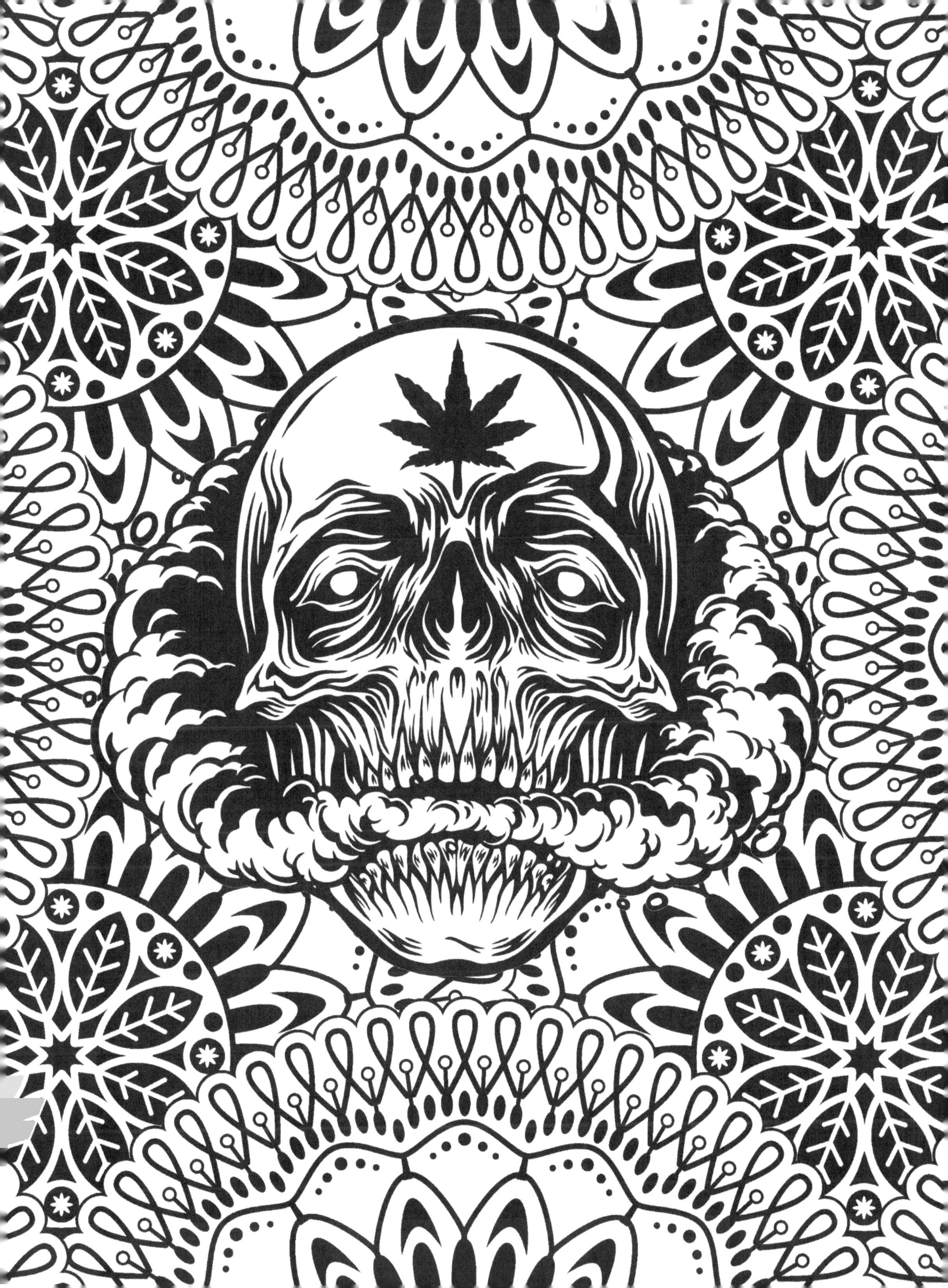

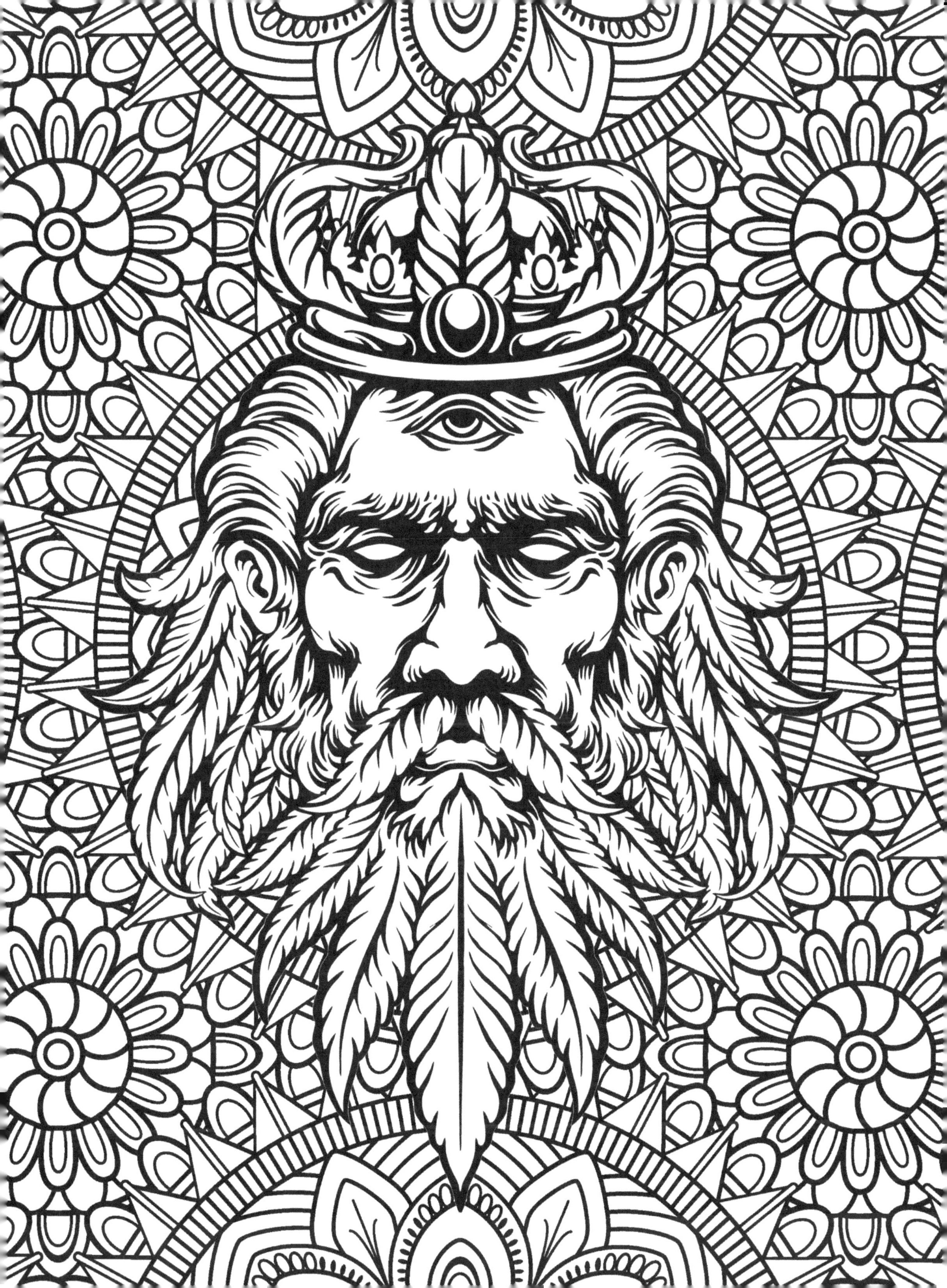

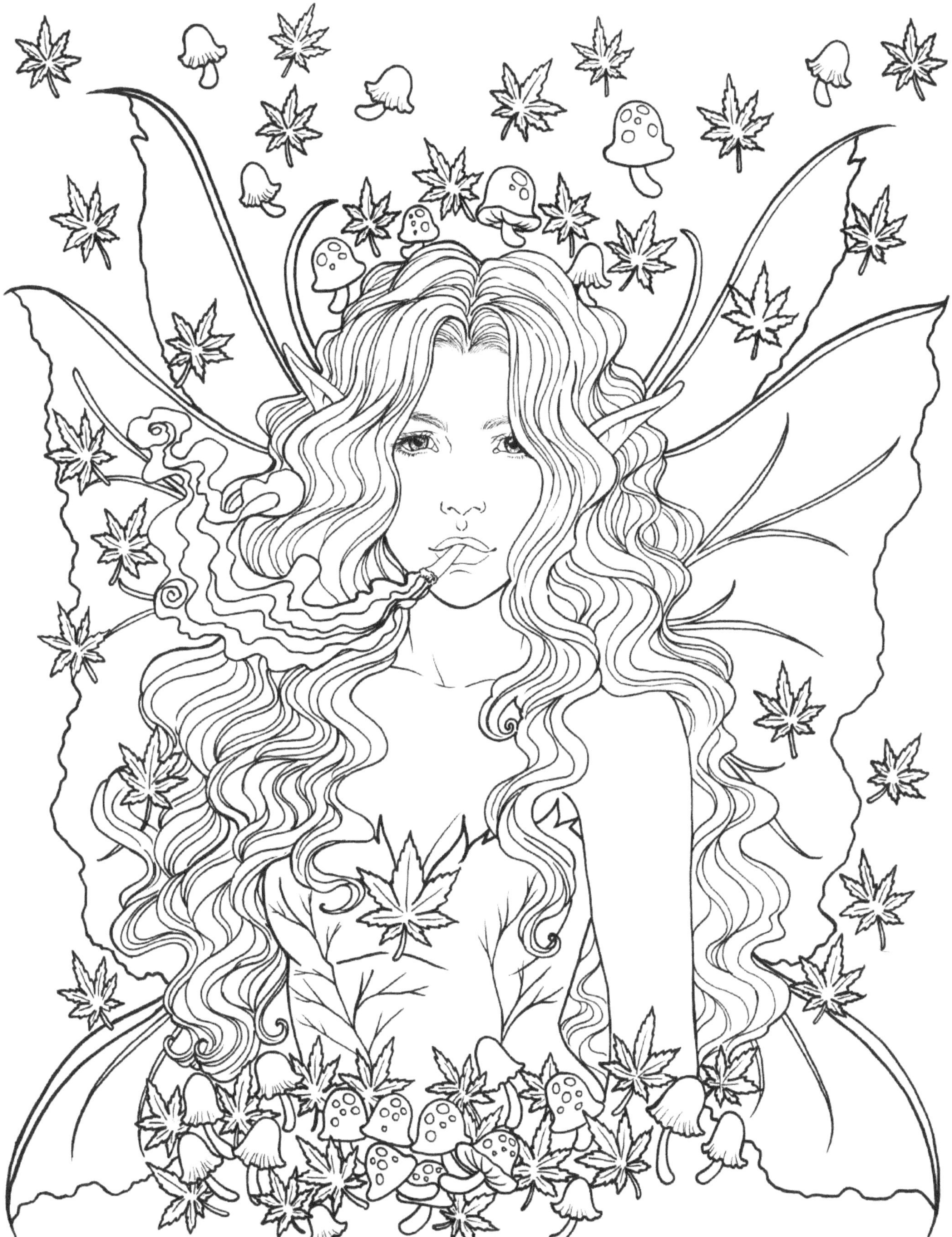

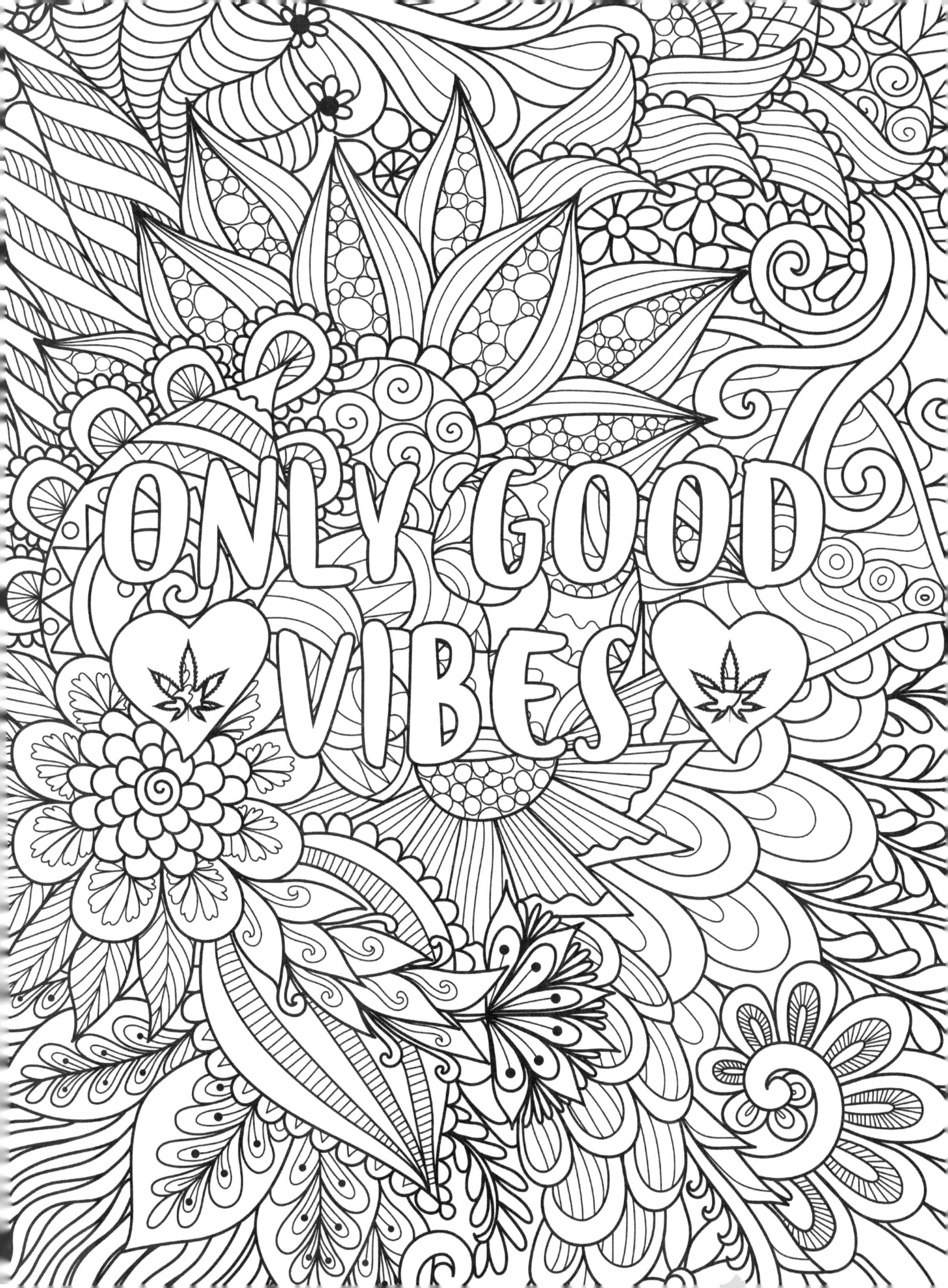
ONLY GOOD
VIBES

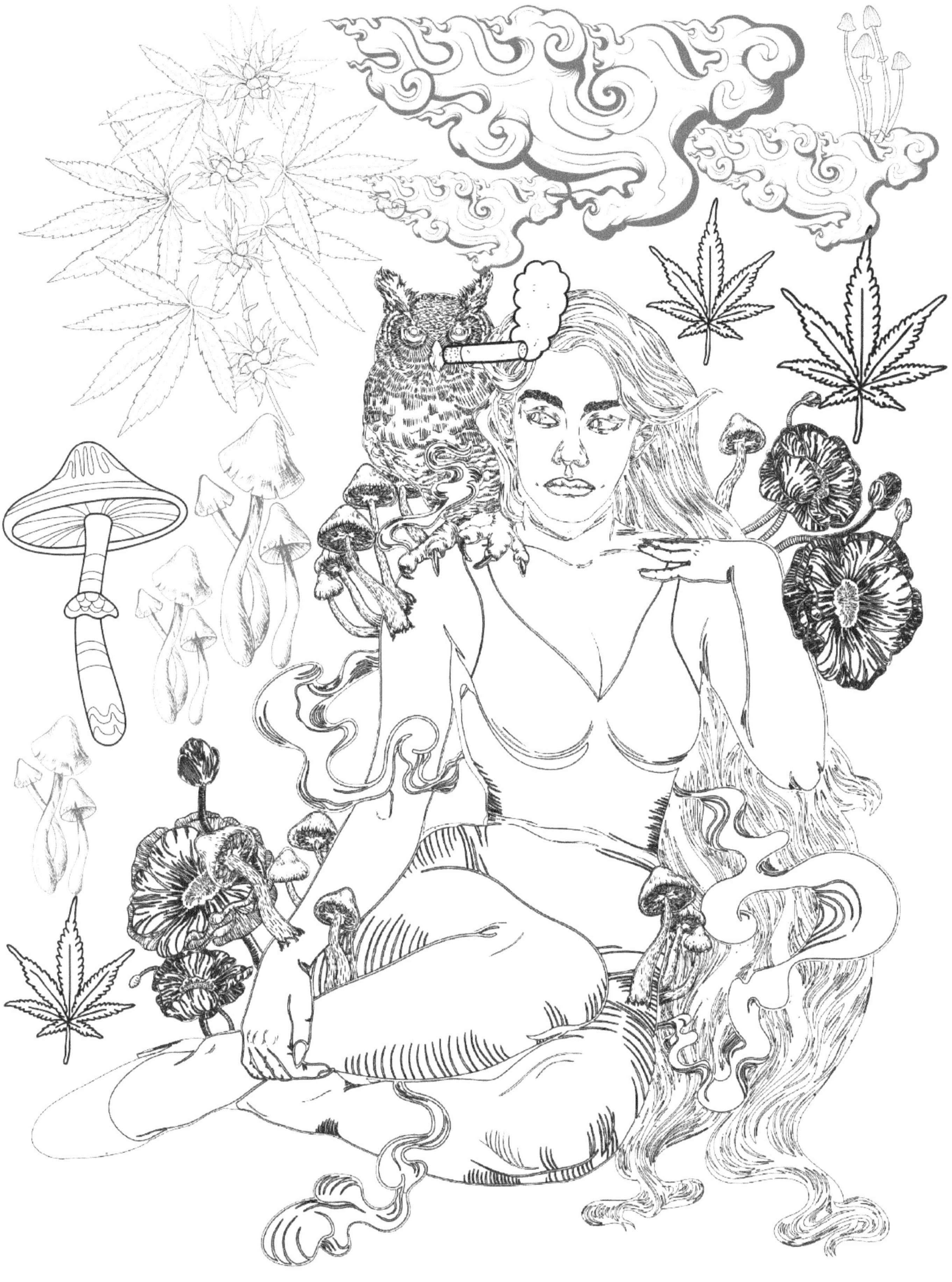

IT'S
4:20
SOMEWHERE

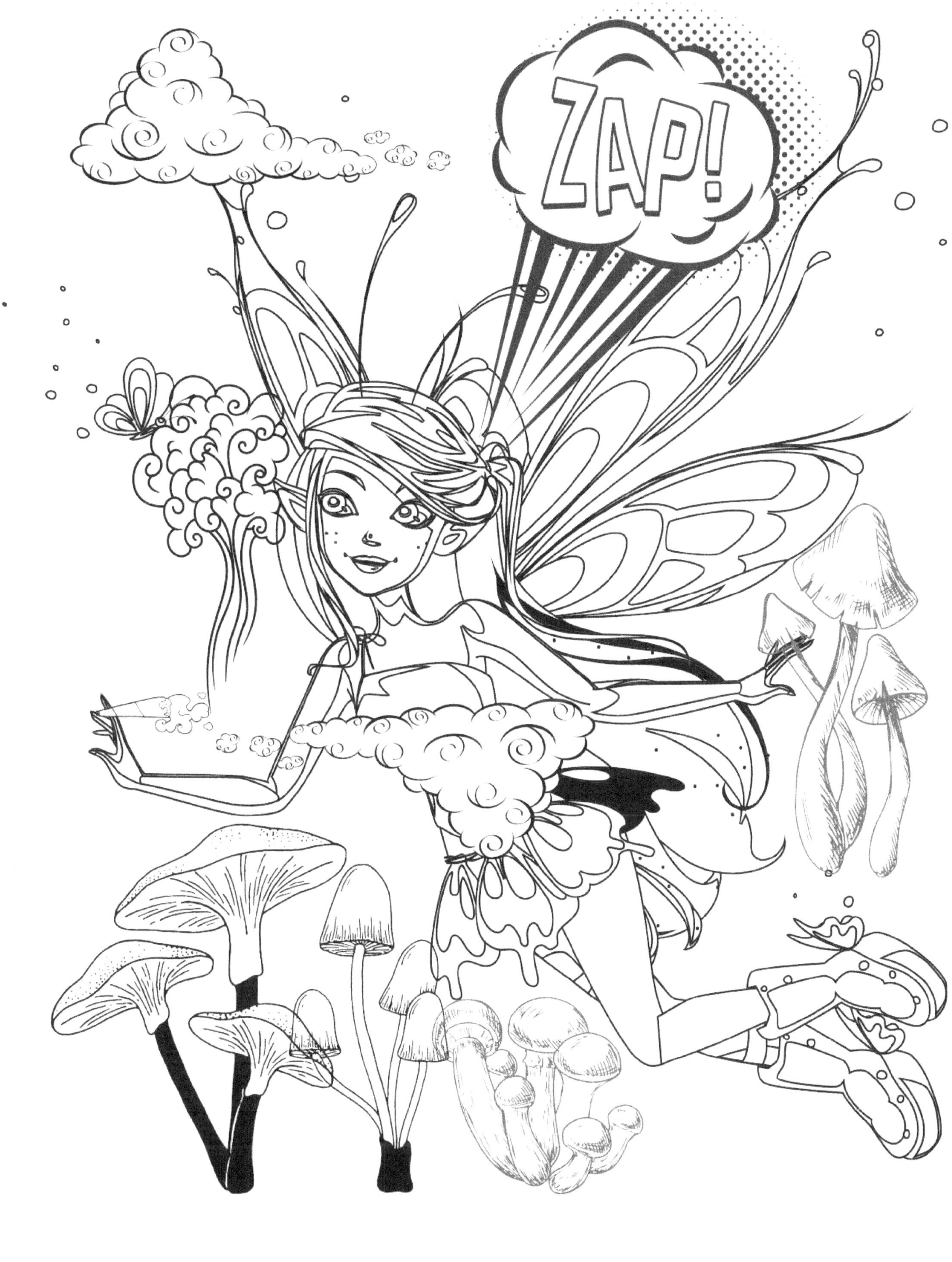
ZAP!

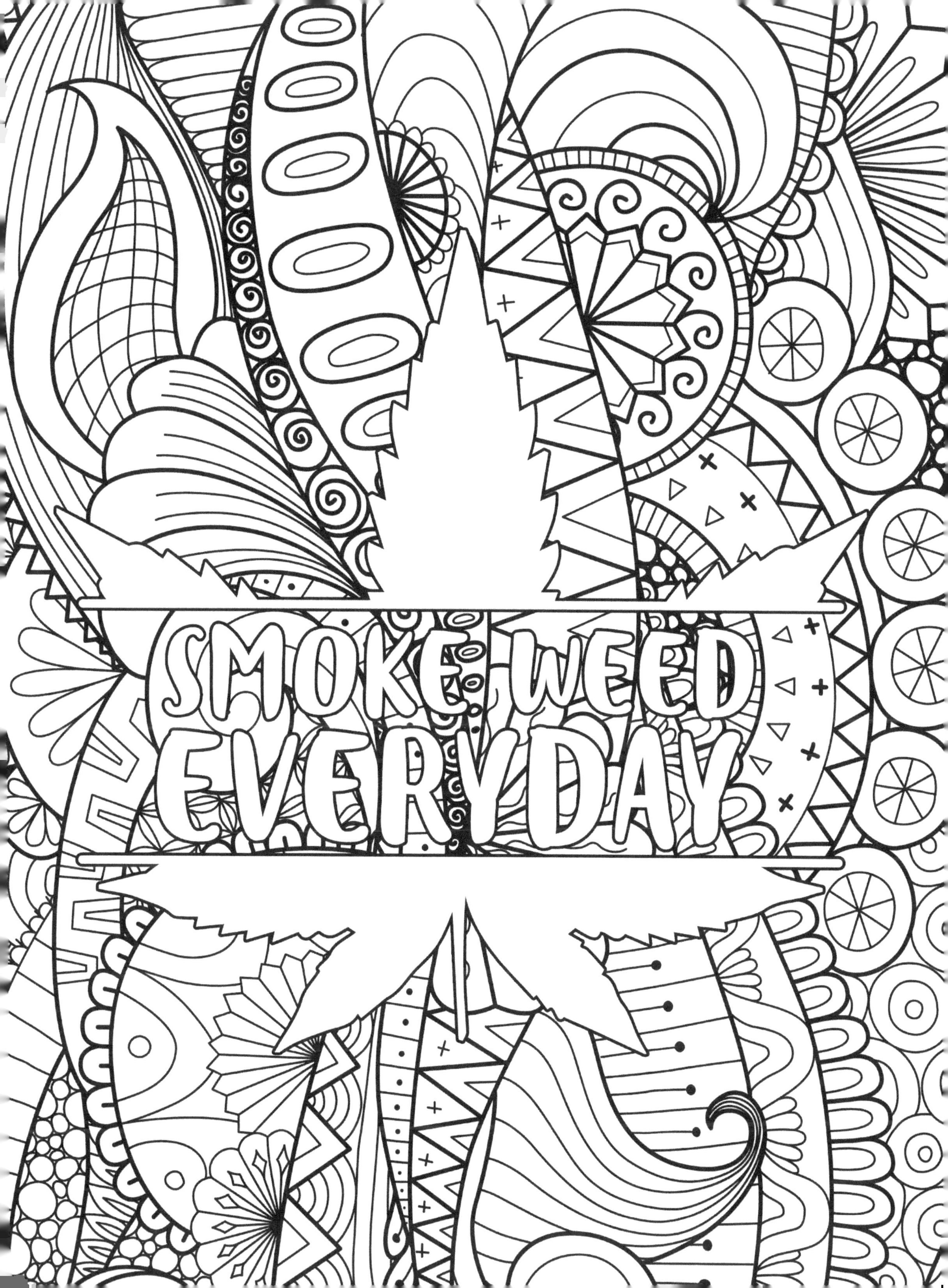
SMOKE WEED
EVERYDAY

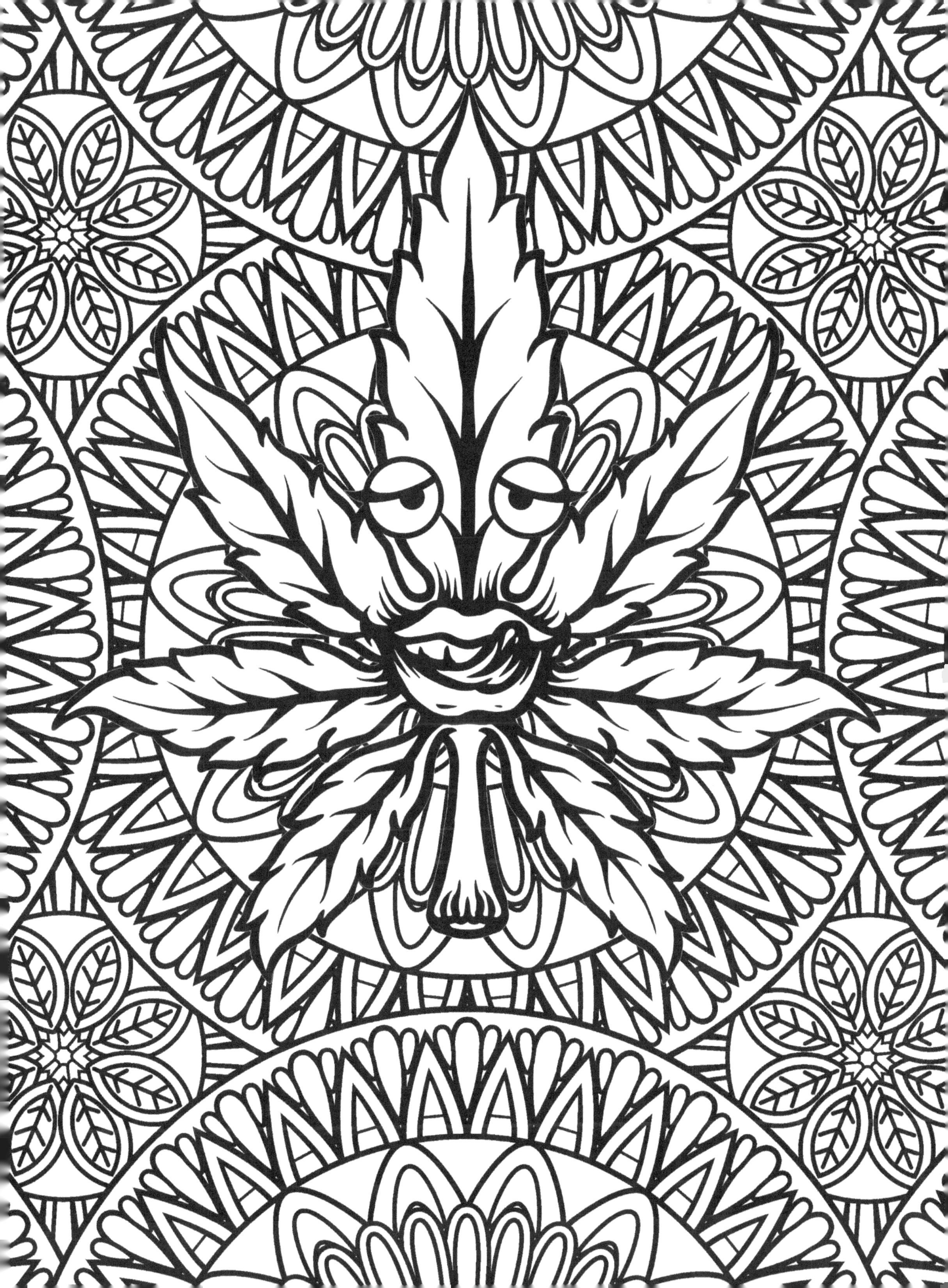

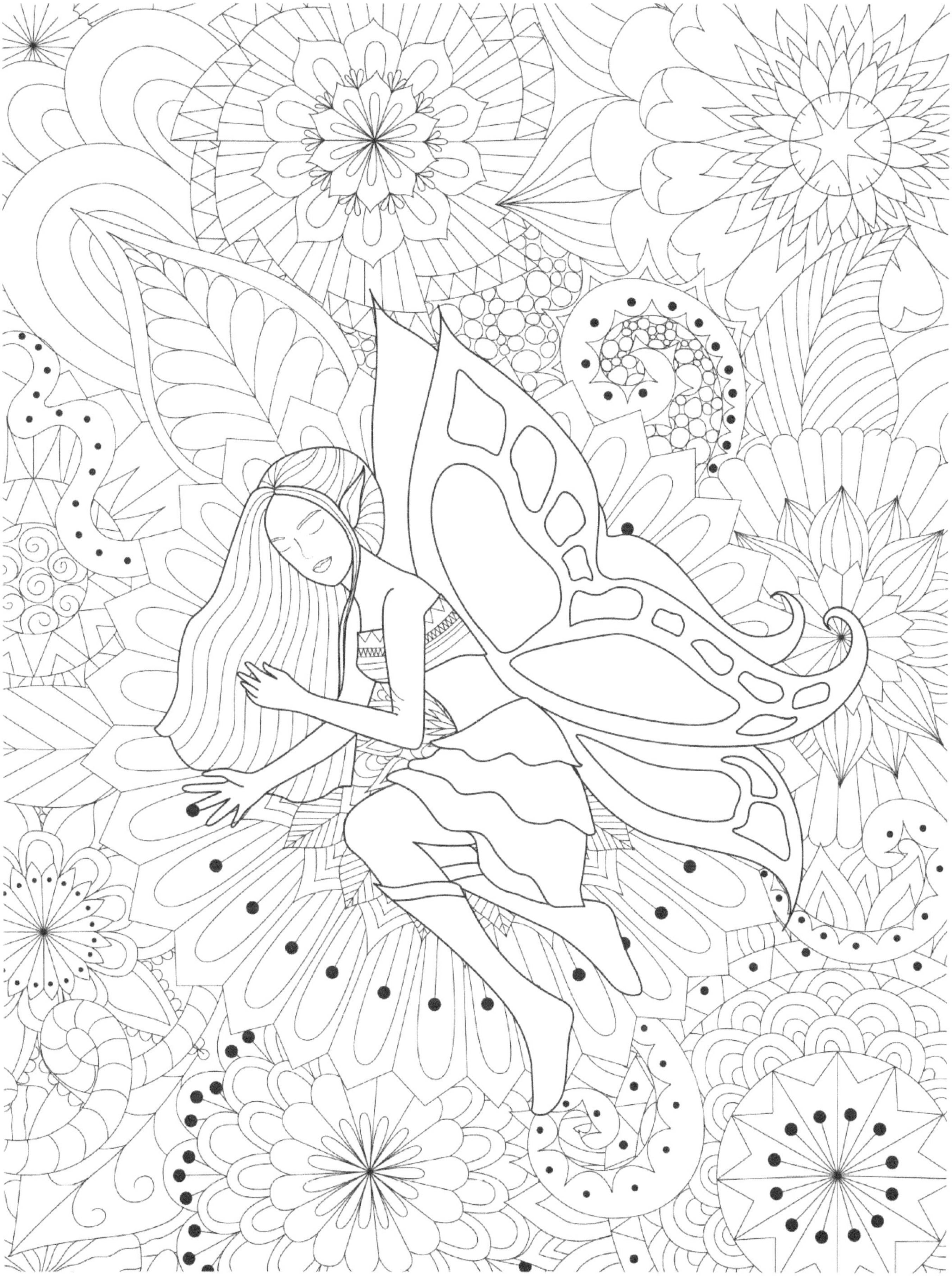

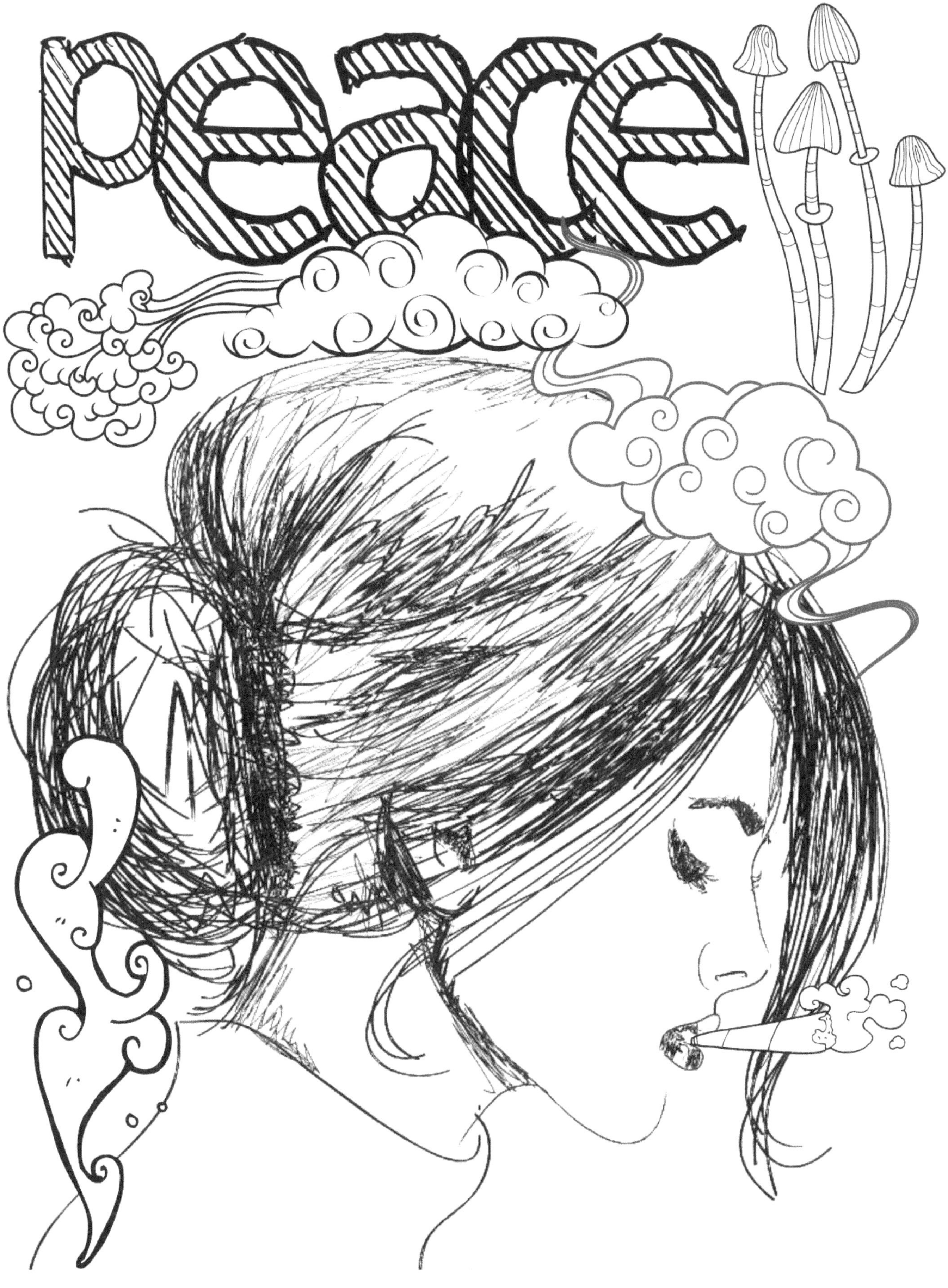
peace

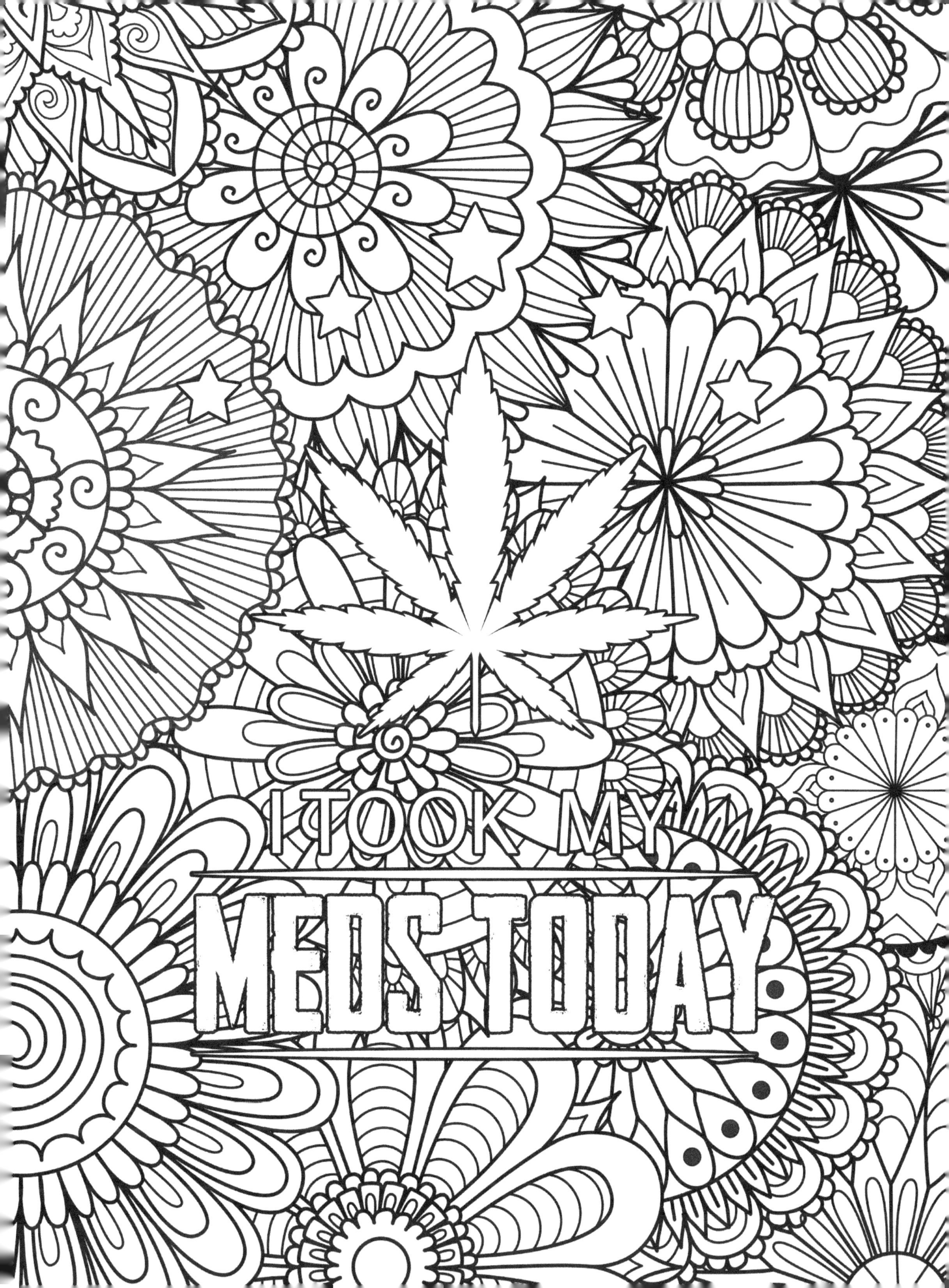
I TOOK MY
MEDS TODAY

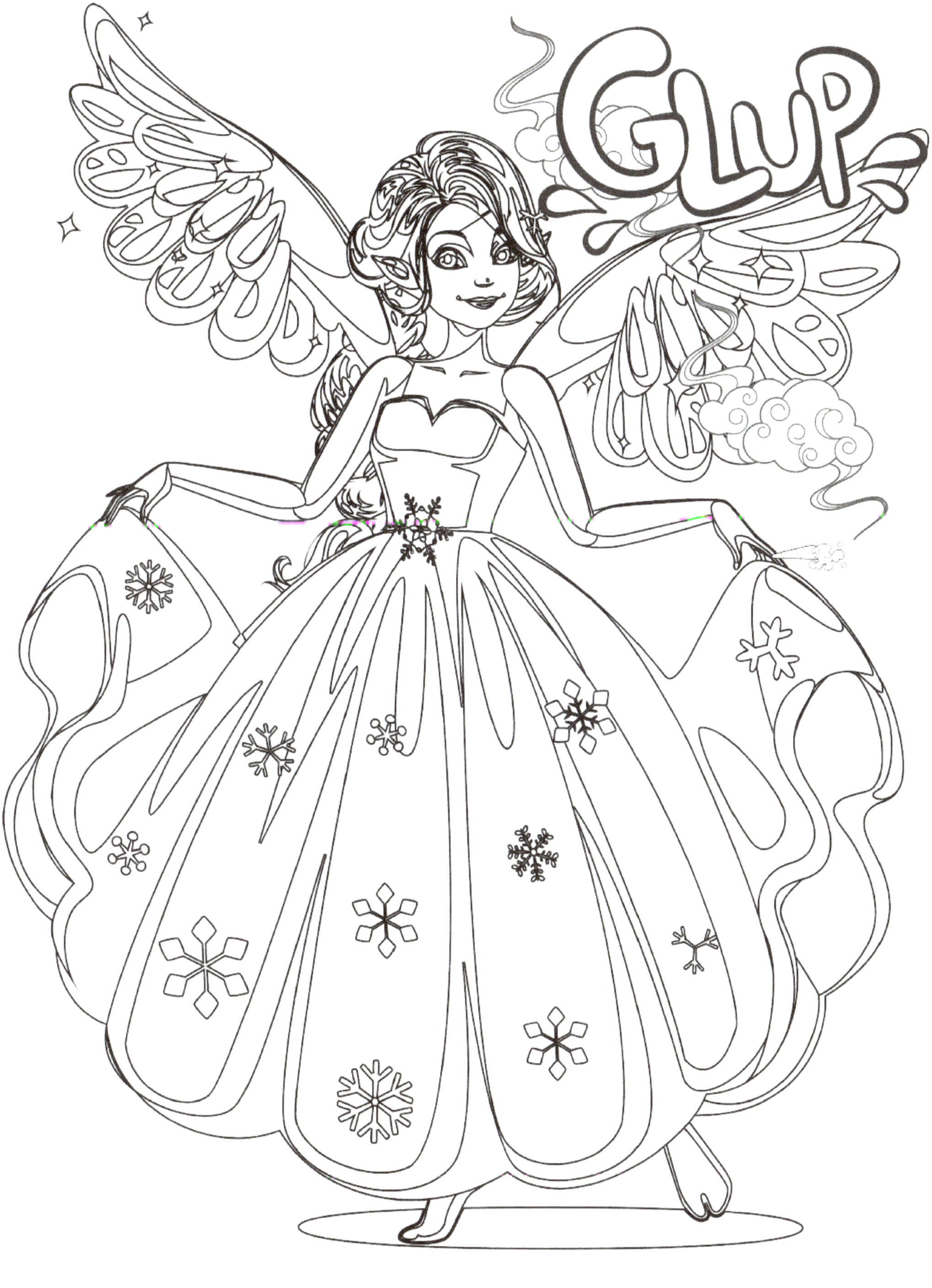
GLUP

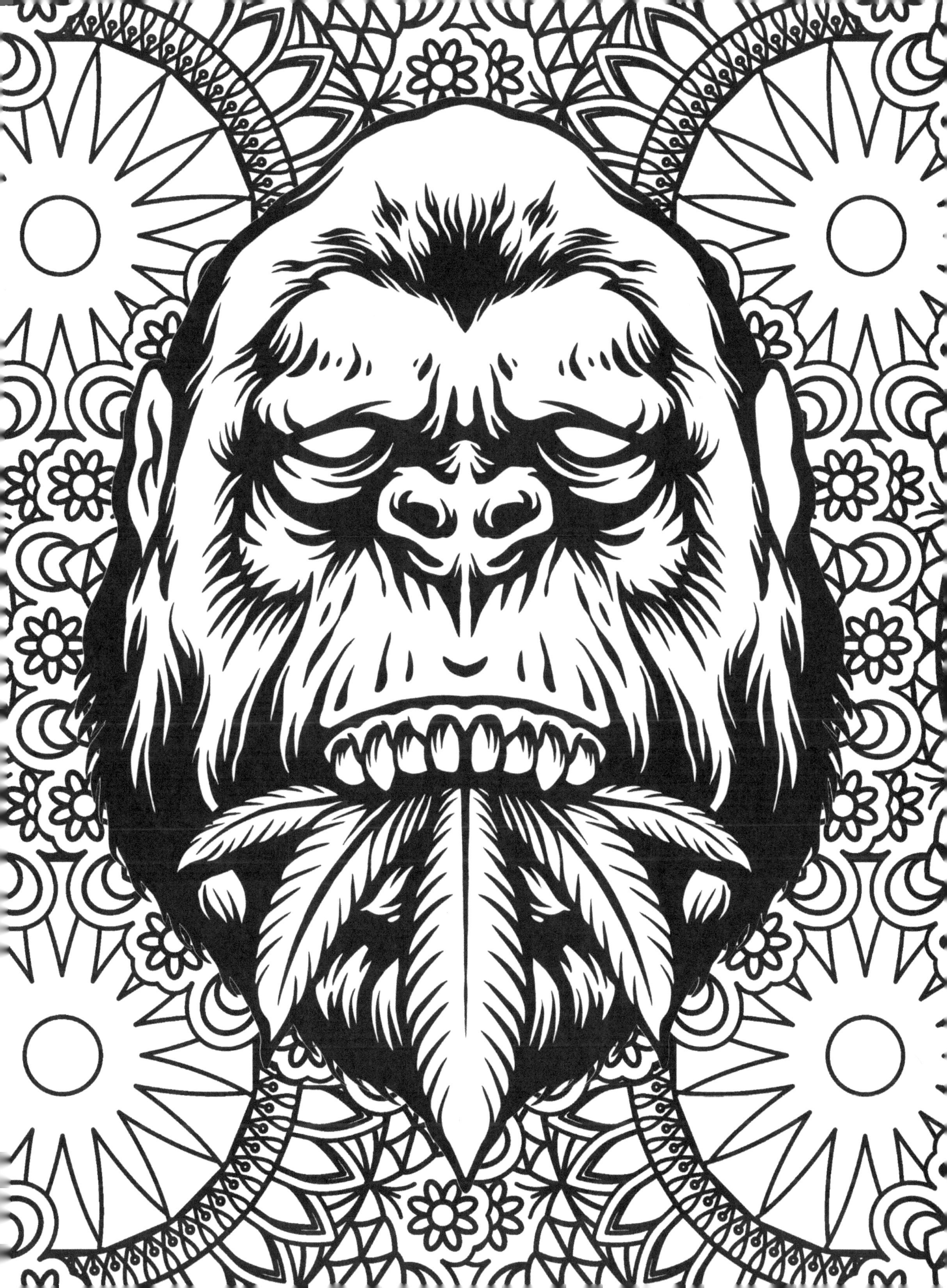

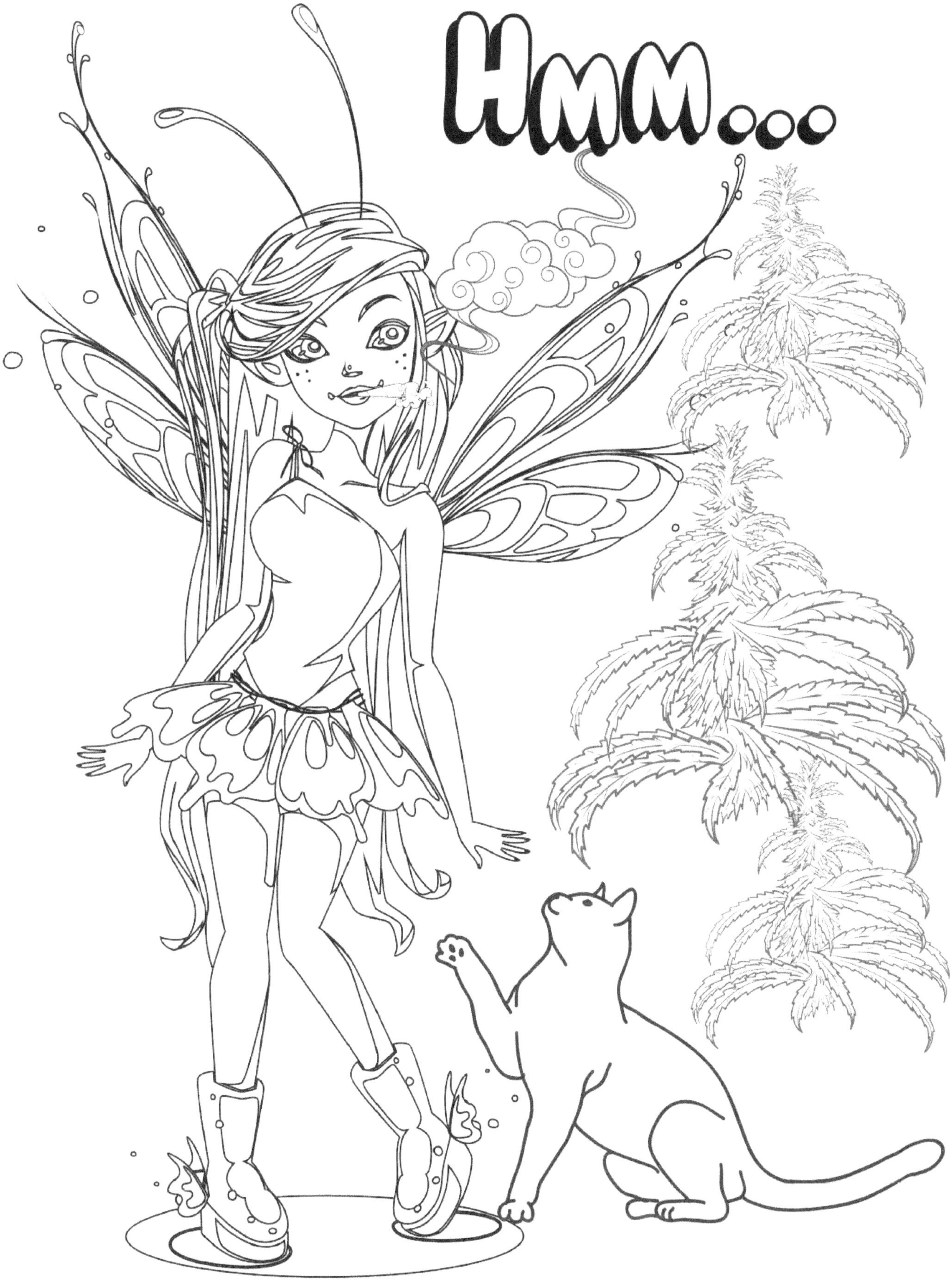
Hmm...

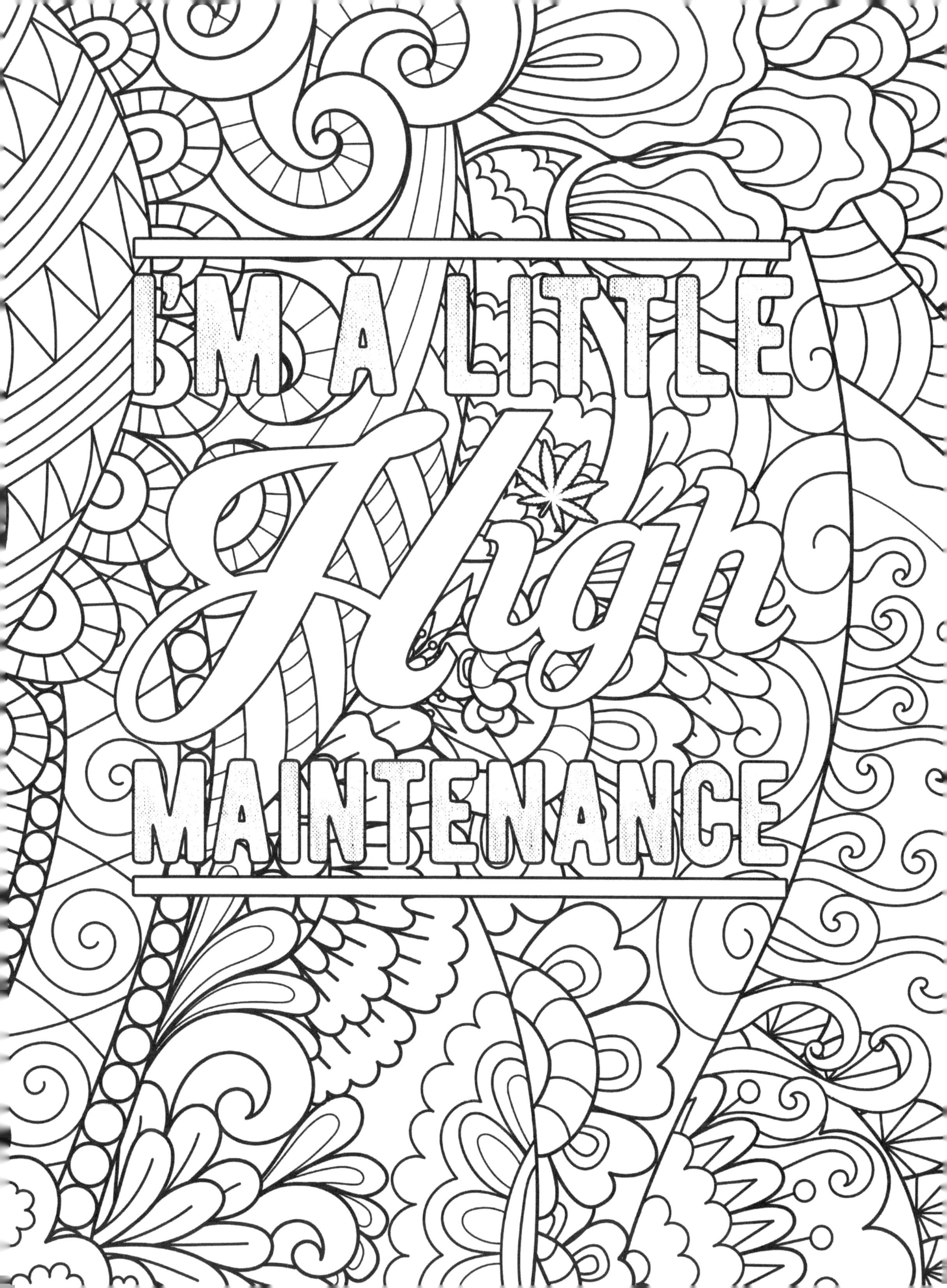
I'M A LITTLE
High
MAINTENANCE

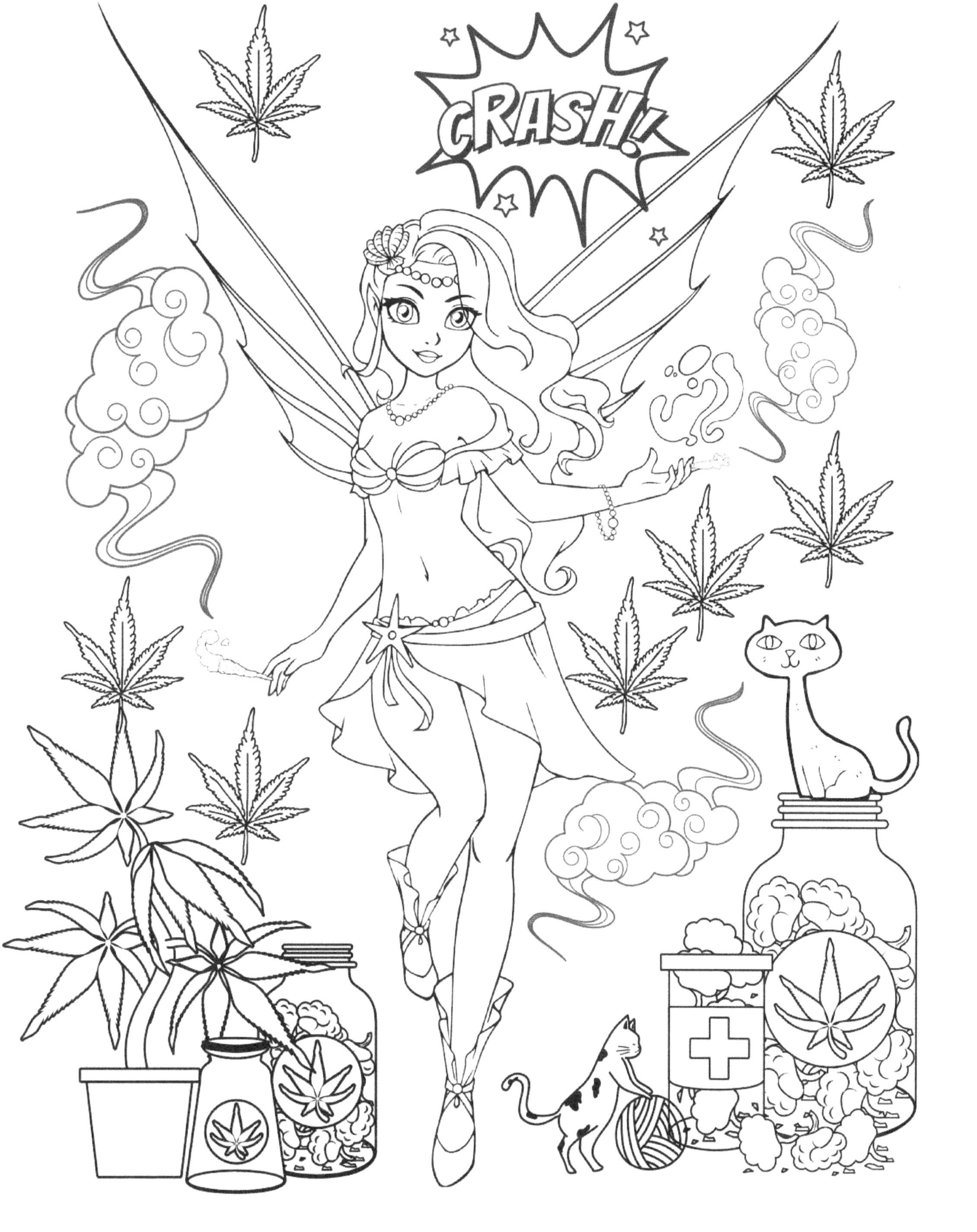
CRASH!

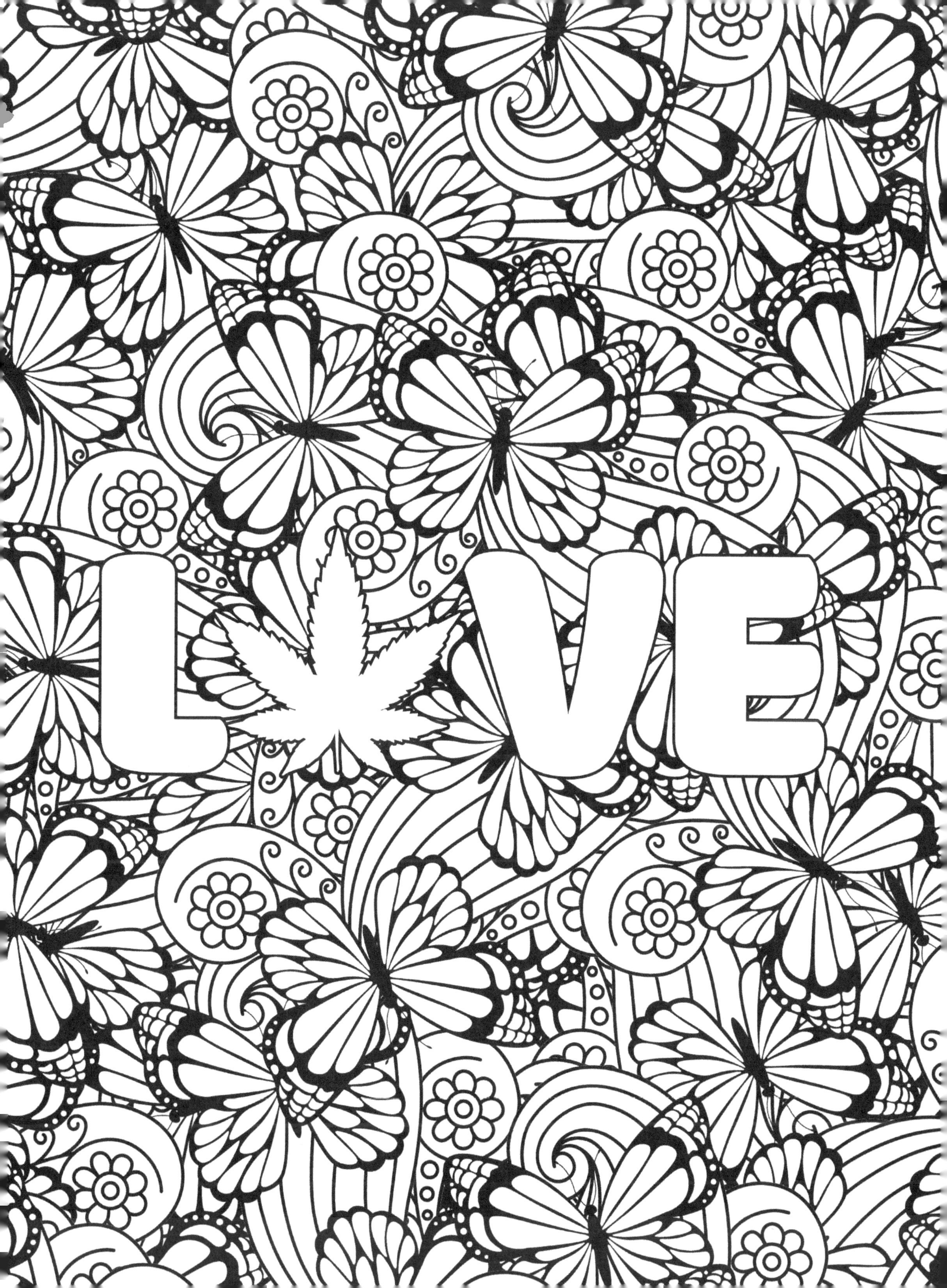
LOVE

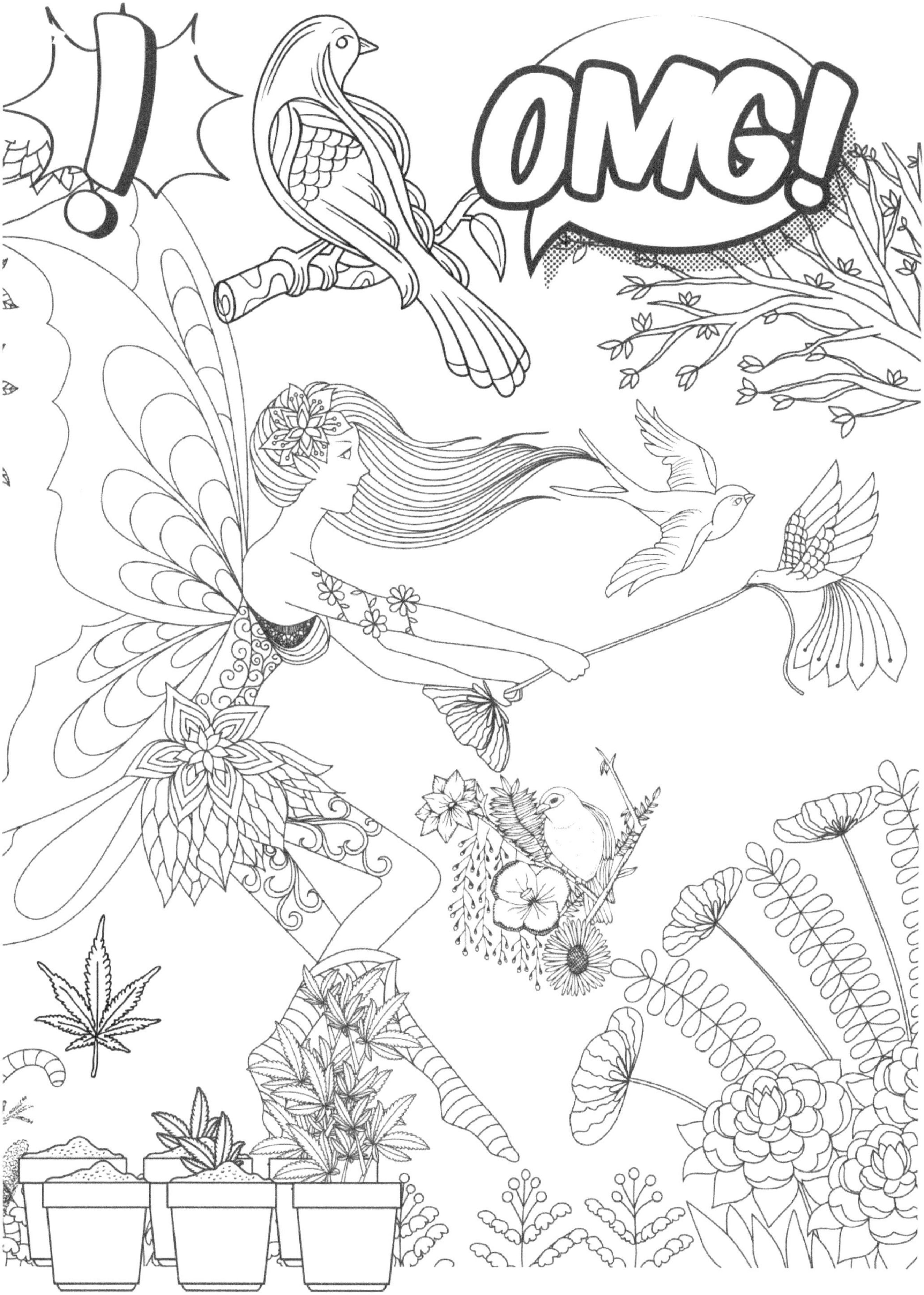

!
OMG!

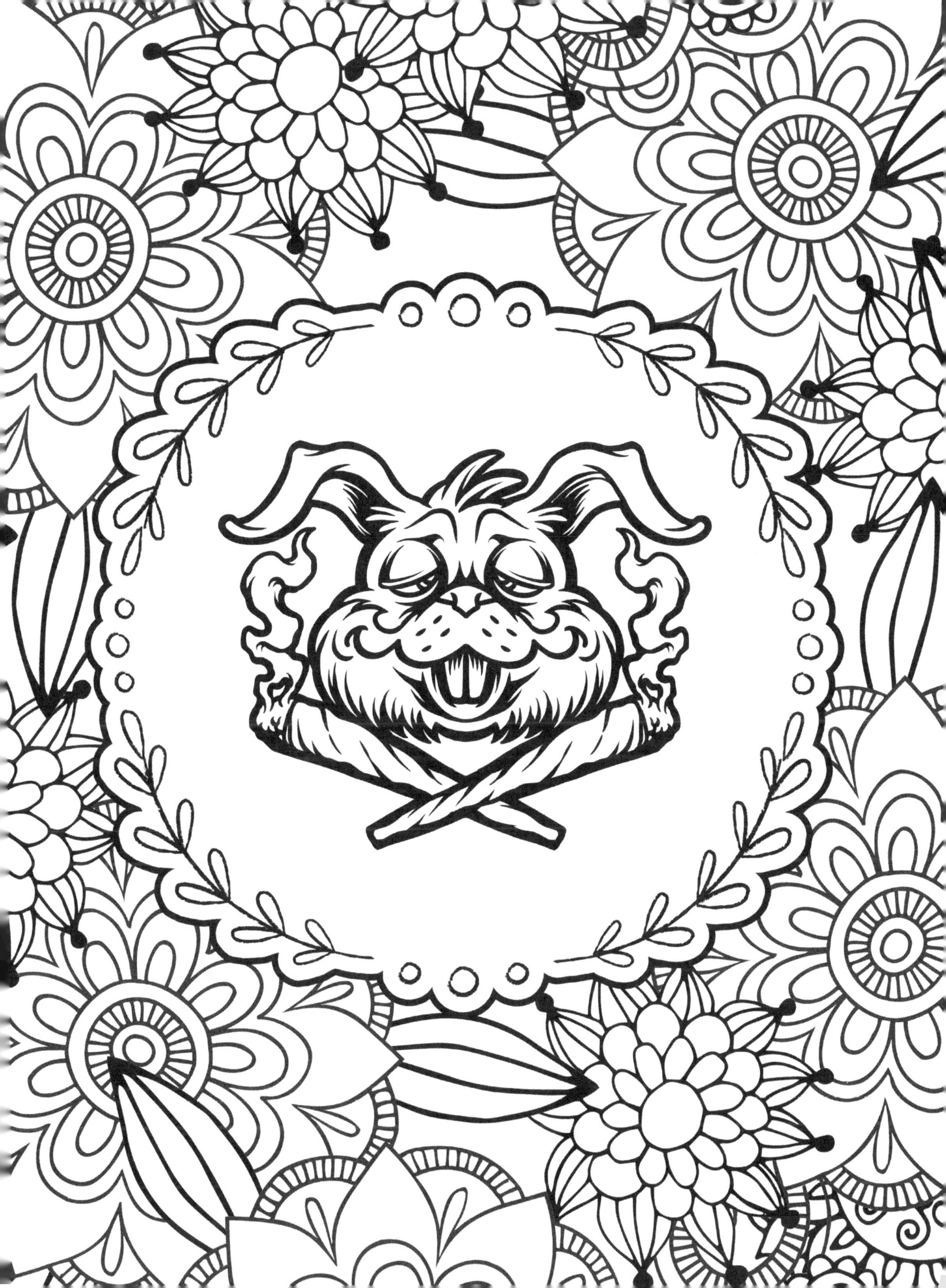

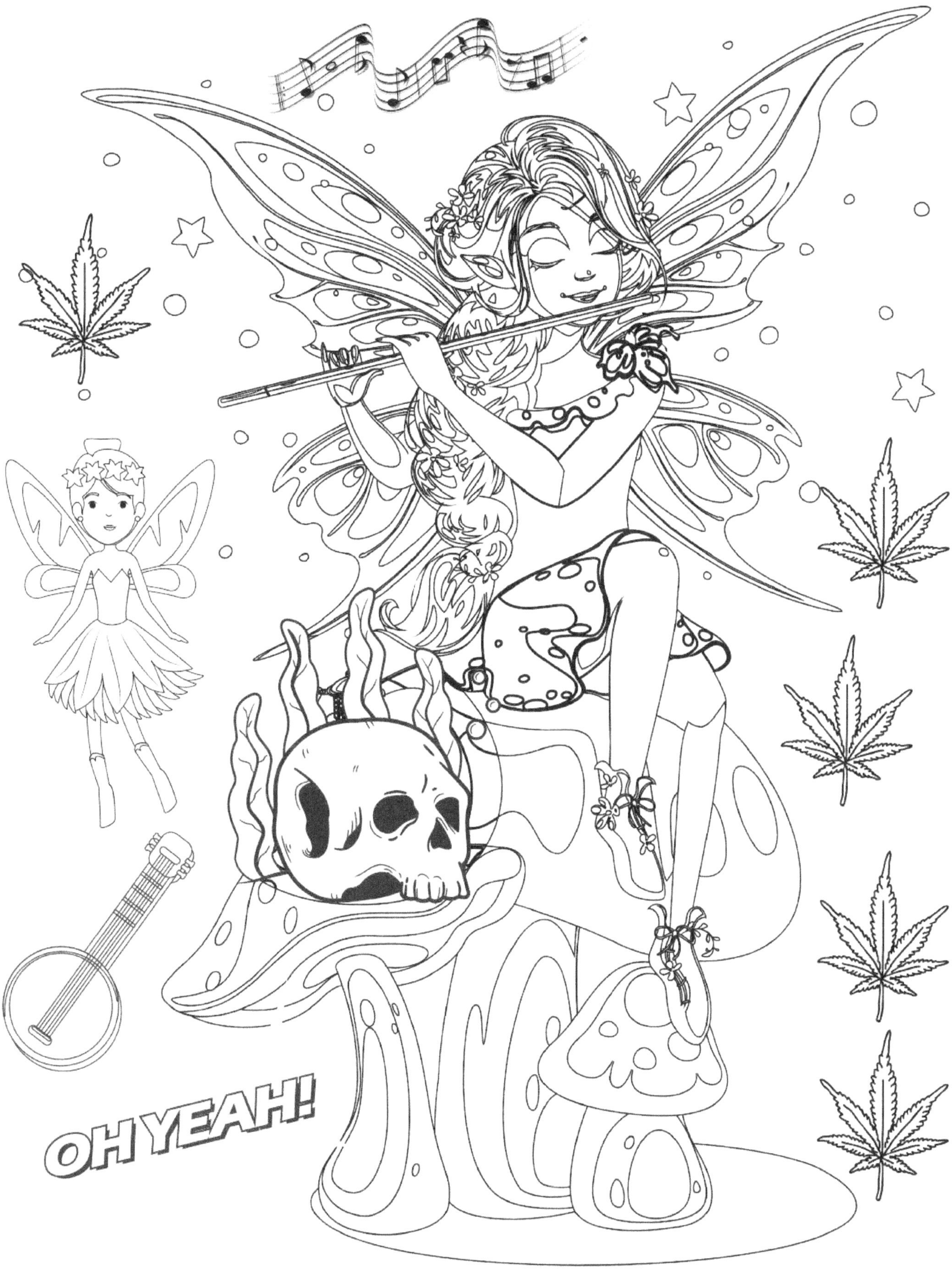
OH YEAH!

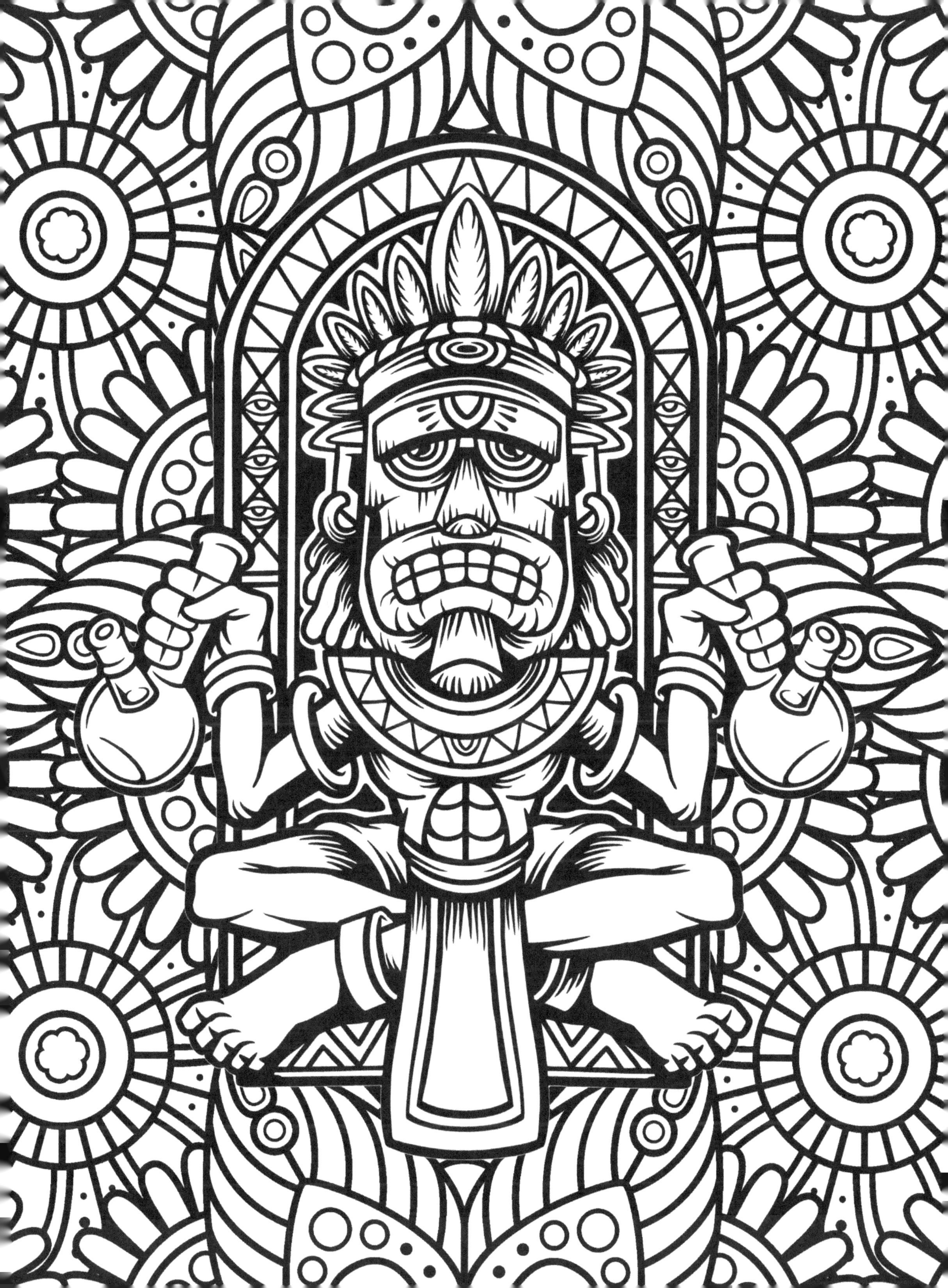

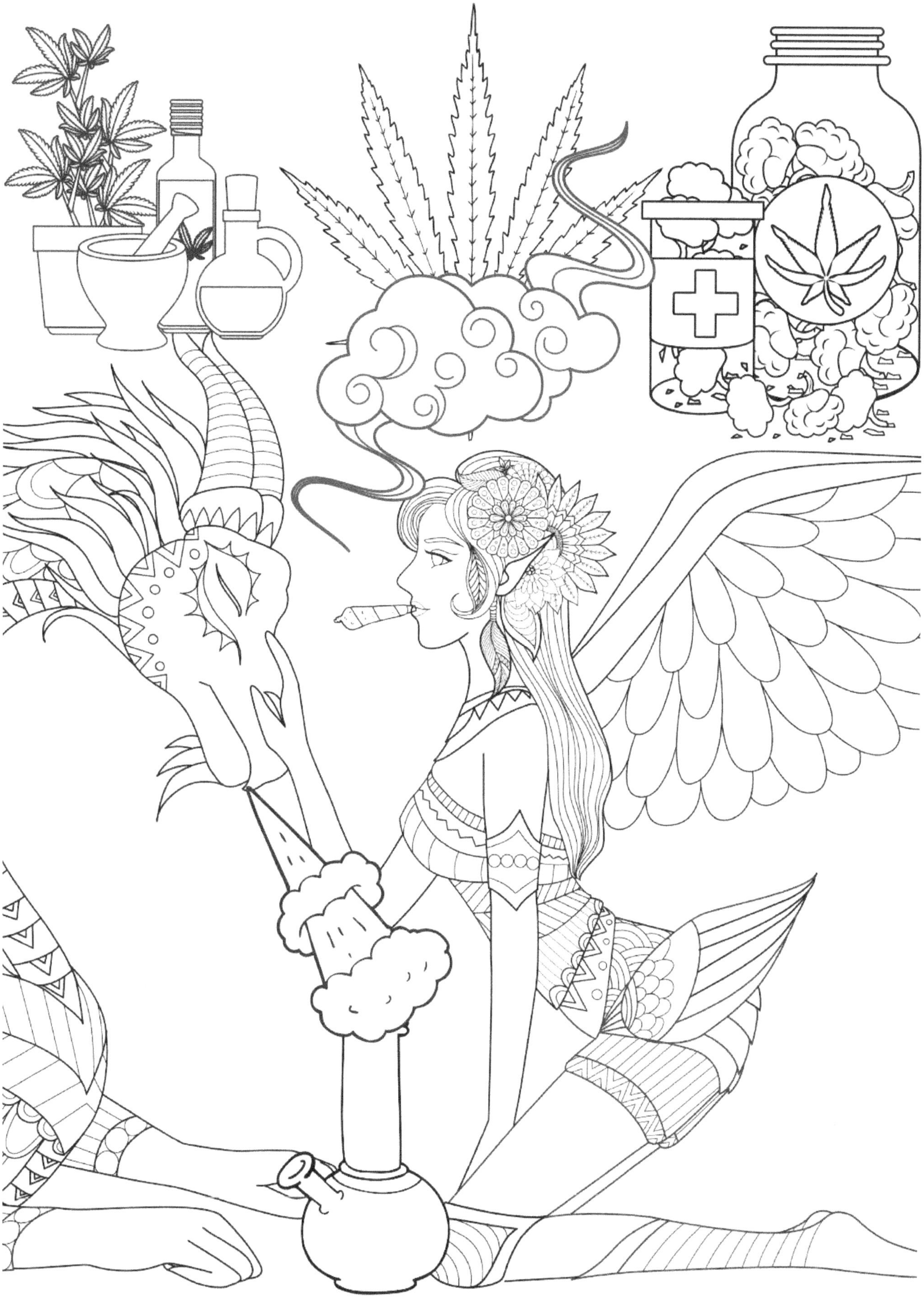

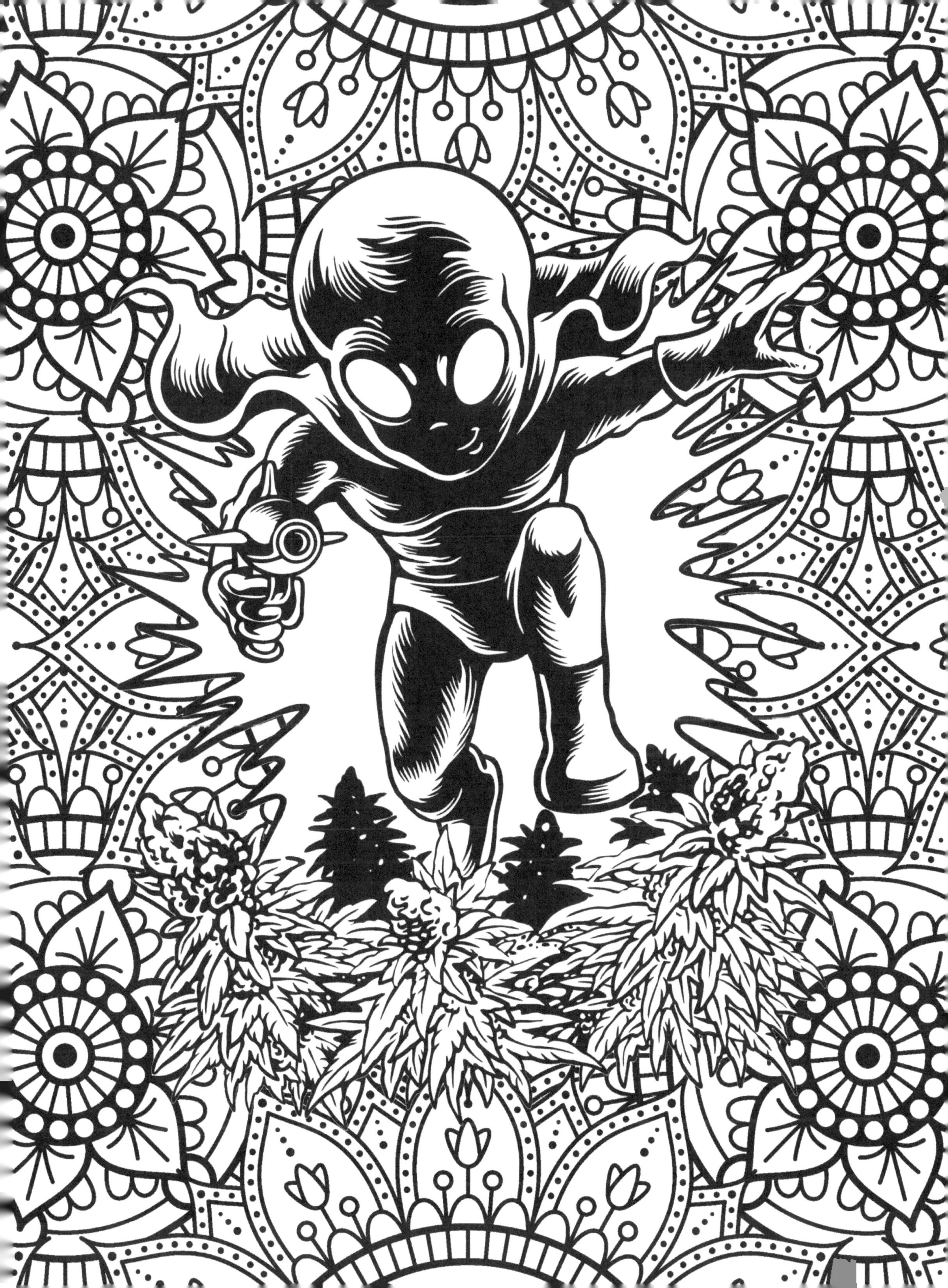

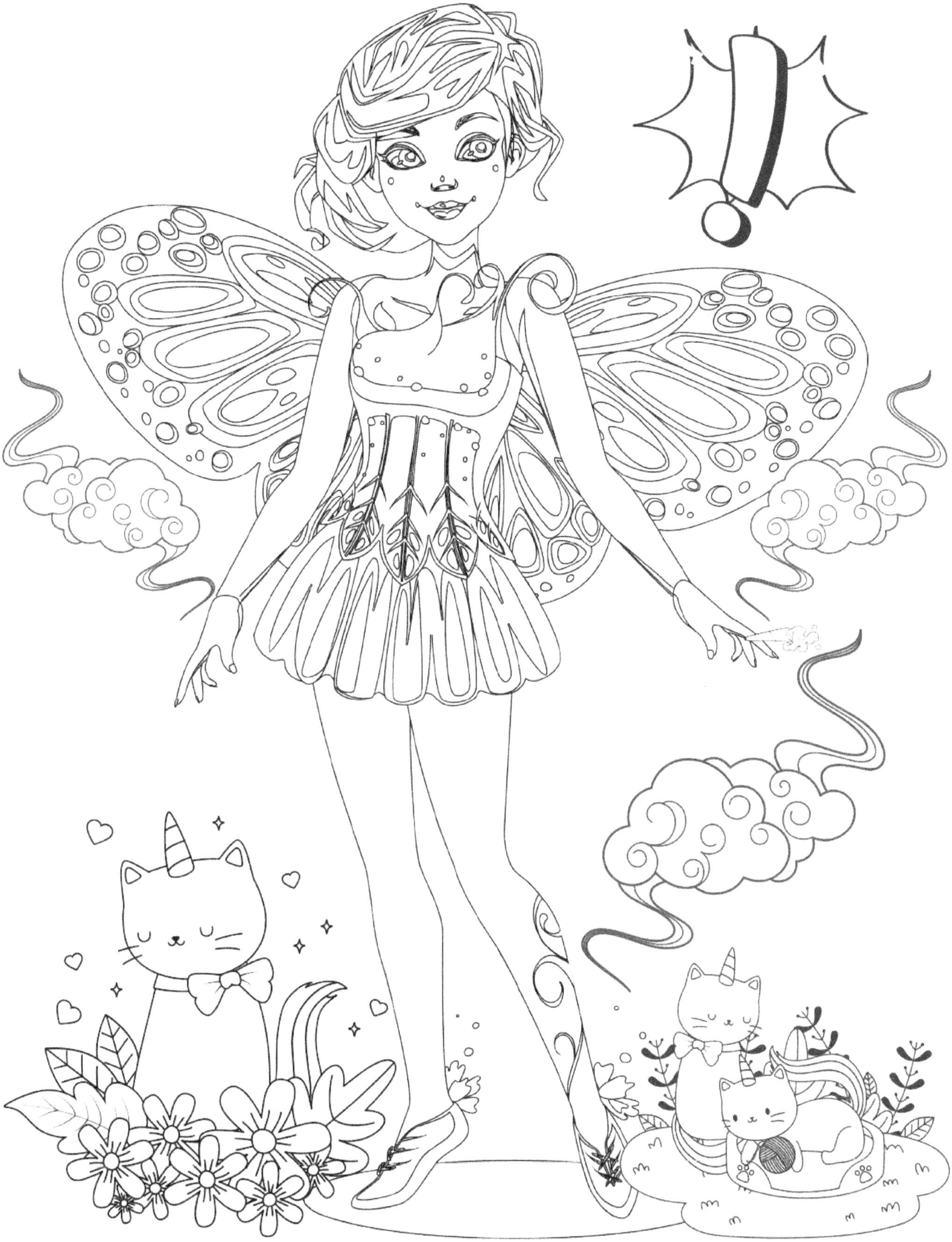

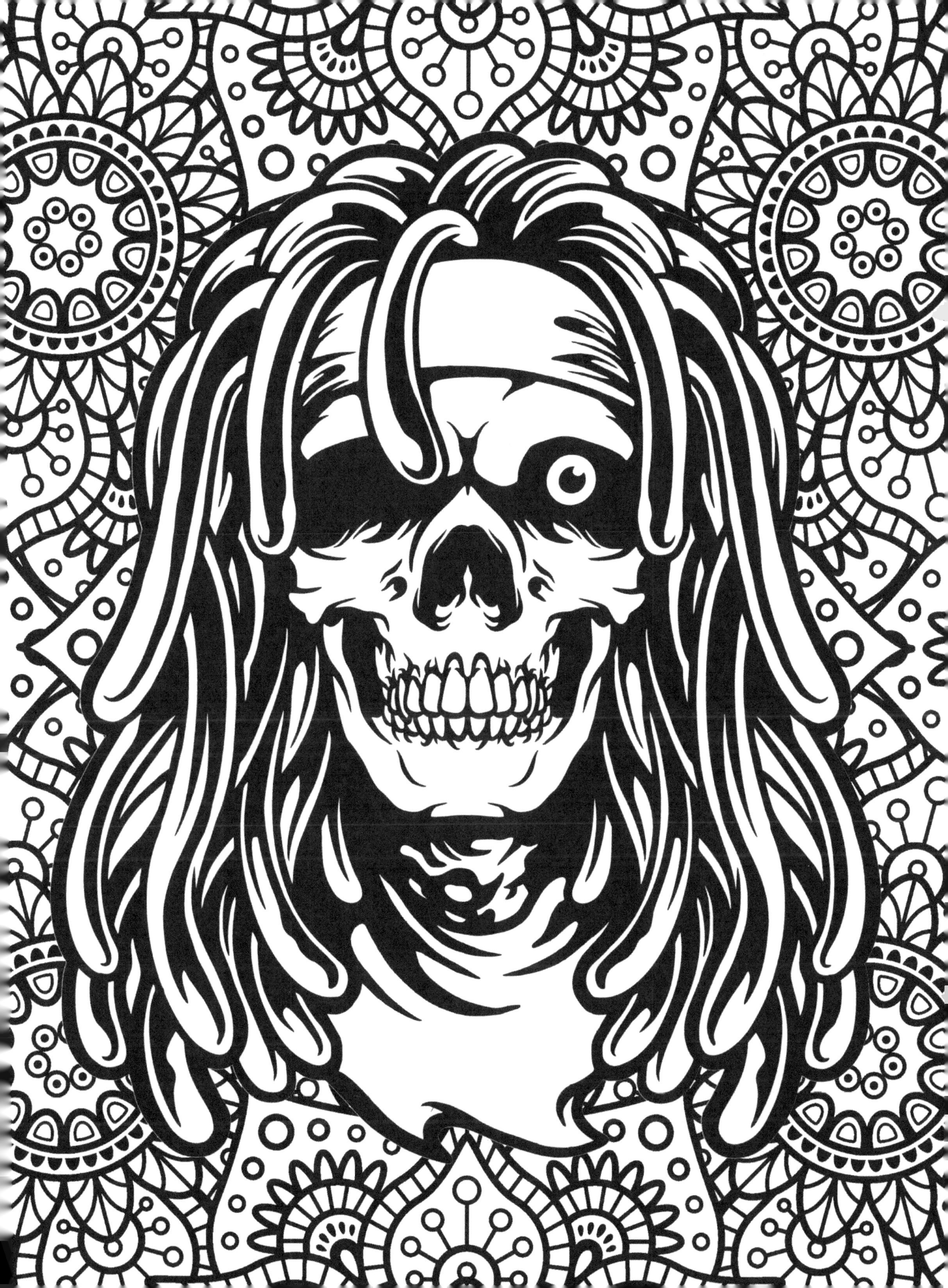

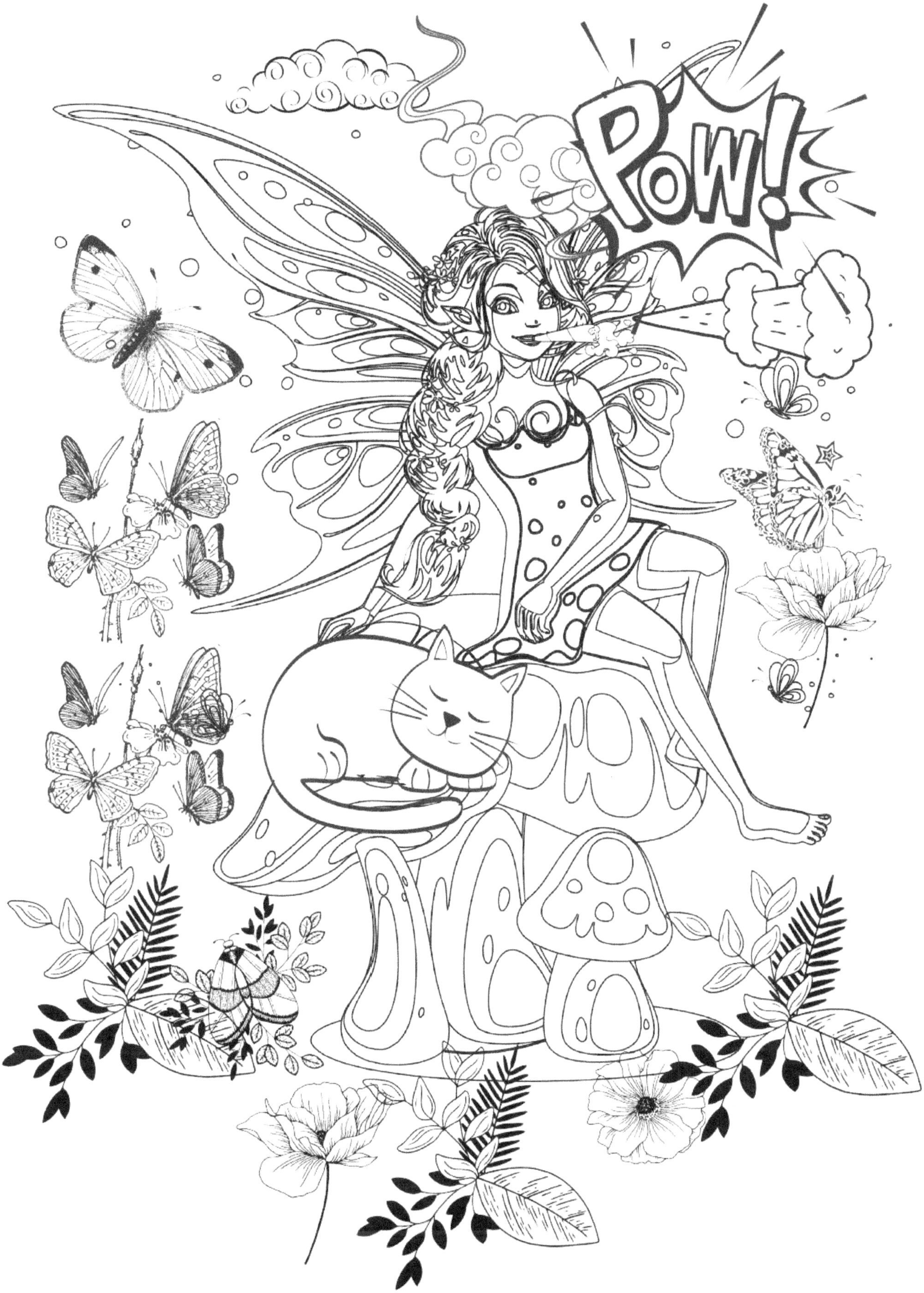
POW!

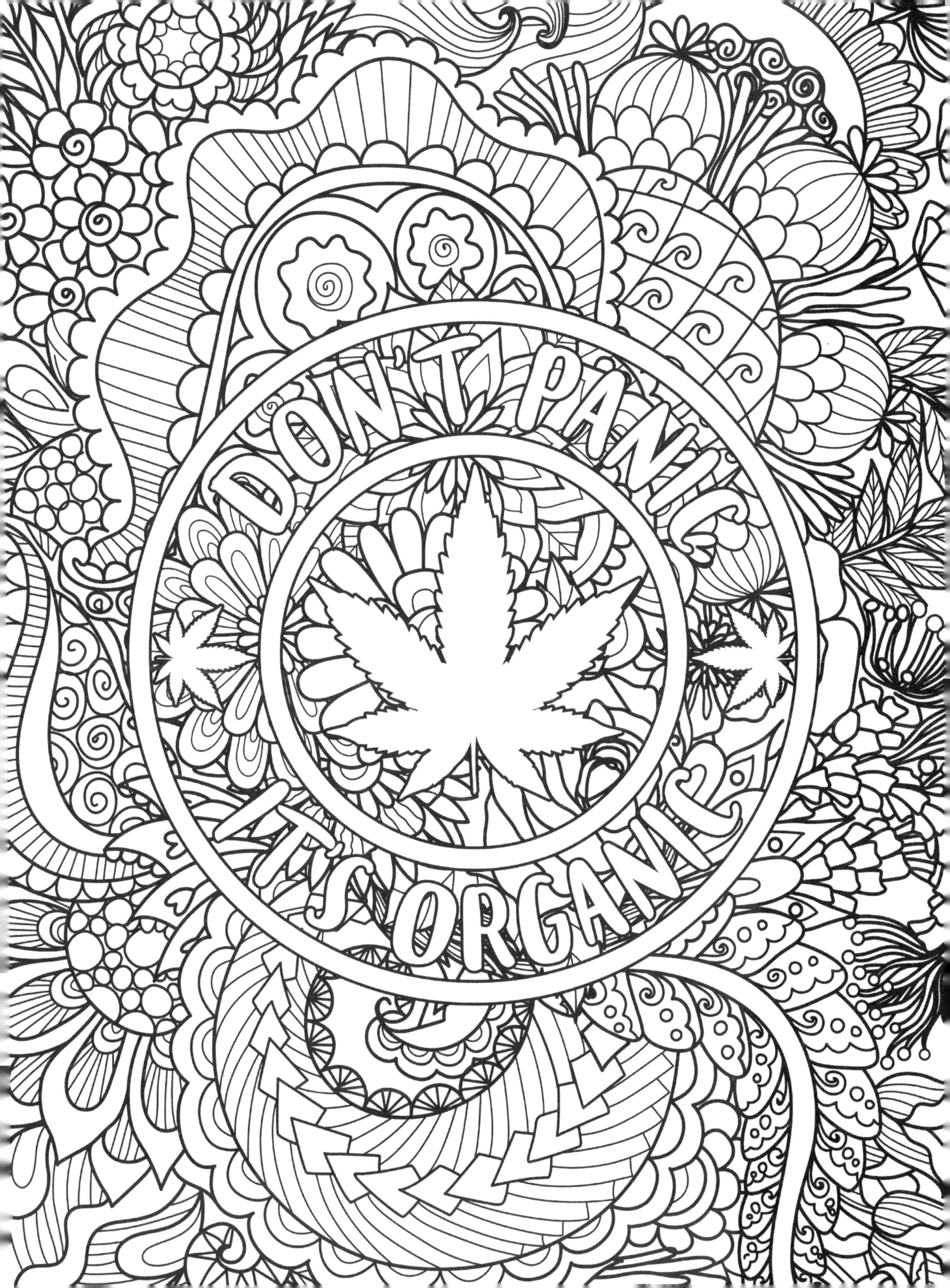
DON'T PANIC
IT'S ORGANIC

www.ingramcontent.com/pod-product-compliance
Lightning Source LLC
Chambersburg PA
CBHW080959220526
45467CB00008B/2622
9798720914998